CHARLES STEWART PARNELL

CHARLES STEWART PARNELL

John Haney

CHELSEA HOUSE PUBLISHERS
NEW YORK
PHILADELPHIA

Chelsea House Publishers
EDITOR-IN-CHIEF: Nancy Toff
EXECUTIVE EDITOR: Remmel T. Nunn
MANAGING EDITOR: Karyn Gullen Browne
COPY CHIEF: Juliann Barbato
PICTURE EDITOR: Adrian G. Allen
ART DIRECTOR: Maria Epes
MANUFACTURING MANAGER: Gerald Levine

World Leaders—Past & Present
SENIOR EDITOR: John W. Selfridge

Staff for CHARLES STEWART PARNELL
ASSISTANT EDITOR: Terrance Dolan
COPY EDITOR: Lisa Fenev
DEPUTY COPY CHIEF: Ellen Scordato
EDITORIAL ASSISTANT: Heather Lewis
PICTURE RESEARCHER: Lisa Kirschner
ASSISTANT ART DIRECTOR: Loraine Machlin
DESIGNER: David Murray
DESIGN ASSISTANT: James Baker
PRODUCTION COORDINATOR: Joseph Romano
COVER ILLUSTRATION: Bill Donahey

First Printing

1 3 5 7 9 8 6 4 2

Library of Congress Cataloging-in-Publication Data

Haney, John.
  Charles Stewart Parnell / John Haney.
  p.   cm.—(World leaders past & present)
  Bibliography: p.
  Includes index.
  Summary: A biography of an Irish Nationalist leader who fought
hard for home rule for Ireland.
  ISBN 1-55546-820-9
       0-7910-0702-2 (pbk.)
  1. Parnell, Charles Stewart, 1846–91—Juvenile literature.
2. Politicians—Ireland—Biography—Juvenile literature.
3. Nationalists—Ireland—Biography—Juvenile literature. 4. Home
rule (Ireland)—Juvenile literature. 5. Ireland—Politics and
government—19th century—Juvenile literature. [1. Parnell, Charles
Stewart, 1846–91. 2. Politicians. 3. Ireland—Biography.] I. Title.
II. Series.
DA958.P2H27   1989
941.5081′092′4—dc19   88-32983
[B]   CIP
[92]   AC

Contents

John Adams
John Quincy Adams
Konrad Adenauer
Alexander the Great
Salvador Allende
Marc Antony
Corazon Aquino
Yasir Arafat
King Arthur
Hafez al-Assad
Kemal Atatürk
Attila
Clement Attlee
Augustus Caesar
Menachem Begin
David Ben-Gurion
Otto von Bismarck
Léon Blum
Simon Bolívar
Cesare Borgia
Willy Brandt
Leonid Brezhnev
Julius Caesar
John Calvin
Jimmy Carter
Fidel Castro
Catherine the Great
Charlemagne
Chiang Kai-Shek
Winston Churchill
Georges Clemenceau
Cleopatra
Constantine the Great
Hernán Cortés
Oliver Cromwell
Georges-Jacques
  Danton
Jefferson Davis
Moshe Dayan
Charles de Gaulle
Eamon De Valera
Eugene Debs
Deng Xiaoping
Benjamin Disraeli
Alexander Dubček
François & Jean-Claude
  Duvalier
Dwight Eisenhower
Eleanor of Aquitaine
Elizabeth i
Faisal
Ferdinand & Isabella
Francisco Franco
Benjamin Franklin

Frederick the Great
Indira Gandhi
Mohandas Gandhi
Giuseppe Garibaldi
Amin & Bashir Gemayel
Genghis Khan
William Gladstone
Mikhail Gorbachev
Ulysses S. Grant
Ernesto "Che" Guevara
Tenzin Gyatso
Alexander Hamilton
Dag Hammarskjöld
Henry viii
Henry of Navarre
Paul von Hindenburg
Hirohito
Adolf Hitler
Ho Chi Minh
King Hussein
Ivan the Terrible
Andrew Jackson
James i
Wojciech Jaruzelski
Thomas Jefferson
Joan of Arc
Pope John xxiii
Pope John Paul ii
Lyndon Johnson
Benito Juárez
John Kennedy
Robert Kennedy
Jomo Kenyatta
Ayatollah Khomeini
Nikita Khrushchev
Kim Il Sung
Martin Luther King, Jr.
Henry Kissinger
Kublai Khan
Lafayette
Robert E. Lee
Vladimir Lenin
Abraham Lincoln
David Lloyd George
Louis xiv
Martin Luther
Judas Maccabeus
James Madison
Nelson & Winnie
  Mandela
Mao Zedong
Ferdinand Marcos
George Marshall

Mary, Queen of Scots
Tomáš Masaryk
Golda Meir
Klemens von Metternich
James Monroe
Hosni Mubarak
Robert Mugabe
Benito Mussolini
Napoléon Bonaparte
Gamal Abdel Nasser
Jawaharlal Nehru
Nero
Nicholas II
Richard Nixon
Kwame Nkrumah
Daniel Ortega
Mohammed Reza Pahlavi
Thomas Paine
Charles Stewart
  Parnell
Pericles
Juan Perón
Peter the Great
Pol Pot
Muammar el-Qaddafi
Ronald Reagan
Cardinal Richelieu
Maximilien Robespierre
Eleanor Roosevelt
Franklin Roosevelt
Theodore Roosevelt
Anwar Sadat
Haile Selassie
Prince Sihanouk
Jan Smuts
Joseph Stalin
Sukarno
Sun Yat-sen
Tamerlane
Mother Teresa
Margaret Thatcher
Josip Broz Tito
Toussaint L'Ouverture
Leon Trotsky
Pierre Trudeau
Harry Truman
Queen Victoria
Lech Walesa
George Washington
Chaim Weizmann
Woodrow Wilson
Xerxes
Emiliano Zapata
Zhou Enlai

CHELSEA HOUSE PUBLISHERS

ON LEADERSHIP

Arthur M. Schlesinger, jr.

LEADERSHIP, it may be said, is really what makes the world go round. Love no doubt smooths the passage; but love is a private transaction between consenting adults. Leadership is a public transaction with history. The idea of leadership affirms the capacity of individuals to move, inspire, and mobilize masses of people so that they act together in pursuit of an end. Sometimes leadership serves good purposes, sometimes bad; but whether the end is benign or evil, great leaders are those men and women who leave their personal stamp on history.

Now, the very concept of leadership implies the proposition that individuals can make a difference. This proposition has never been universally accepted. From classical times to the present day, eminent thinkers have regarded individuals as no more than the agents and pawns of larger forces, whether the gods and goddesses of the ancient world or, in the modern era, race, class, nation, the dialectic, the will of the people, the spirit of the times, history itself. Against such forces, the individual dwindles into insignificance.

So contends the thesis of historical determinism. Tolstoy's great novel *War and Peace* offers a famous statement of the case. Why, Tolstoy asked, did millions of men in the Napoleonic Wars, denying their human feelings and their common sense, move back and forth across Europe slaughtering their fellows? "The war," Tolstoy answered, "was bound to happen simply because it was bound to happen." All prior history predetermined it. As for leaders, they, Tolstoy said, "are but the labels that serve to give a name to an end and, like labels, they have the least possible connection with the event." The greater the leader, "the more conspicuous the inevitability and the predestination of every act he commits." The leader, said Tolstoy, is "the slave of history."

Determinism takes many forms. Marxism is the determinism of class. Nazism the determinism of race. But the idea of men and women as the slaves of history runs athwart the deepest human instincts. Rigid determinism abolishes the idea of human freedom—

the assumption of free choice that underlies every move we make, every word we speak, every thought we think. It abolishes the idea of human responsibility, since it is manifestly unfair to reward or punish people for actions that are by definition beyond their control. No one can live consistently by any deterministic creed. The Marxist states prove this themselves by their extreme susceptibility to the cult of leadership.

More than that, history refutes the idea that individuals make no difference. In December 1931 a British politician crossing Park Avenue in New York City between 76th and 77th Streets around 10:30 P.M. looked in the wrong direction and was knocked down by an automobile—a moment, he later recalled, of a man aghast, a world aglare: "I do not understand why I was not broken like an eggshell or squashed like a gooseberry." Fourteen months later an American politician, sitting in an open car in Miami, Florida, was fired on by an assassin; the man beside him was hit. Those who believe that individuals make no difference to history might well ponder whether the next two decades would have been the same had Mario Constasino's car killed Winston Churchill in 1931 and Giuseppe Zangara's bullet killed Franklin Roosevelt in 1933. Suppose, in addition, that Adolf Hitler had been killed in the street fighting during the Munich *Putsch* of 1923 and that Lenin had died of typhus during World War I. What would the 20th century be like now?

For better or for worse, individuals do make a difference. "The notion that a people can run itself and its affairs anonymously," wrote the philosopher William James, "is now well known to be the silliest of absurdities. Mankind does nothing save through initiatives on the part of inventors, great or small, and imitation by the rest of us—these are the sole factors in human progress. Individuals of genius show the way, and set the patterns, which common people then adopt and follow."

Leadership, James suggests, means leadership in thought as well as in action. In the long run, leaders in thought may well make the greater difference to the world. But, as Woodrow Wilson once said, "Those only are leaders of men, in the general eye, who lead in action. . . . It is at their hands that new thought gets its translation into the crude language of deeds." Leaders in thought often invent in solitude and obscurity, leaving to later generations the tasks of imitation. Leaders in action—the leaders portrayed in this series—have to be effective in their own time.

And they cannot be effective by themselves. They must act in response to the rhythms of their age. Their genius must be adapted, in a phrase of William James's, "to the receptivities of the moment." Leaders are useless without followers. "There goes the mob," said the French politician hearing a clamor in the streets. "I am their leader. I must follow them." Great leaders turn the inchoate emotions of the mob to purposes of their own. They seize on the opportunities of their time, the hopes, fears, frustrations, crises, potentialities. They succeed when events have prepared the way for them, when the community is awaiting to be aroused, when they can provide the clarifying and organizing ideas. Leadership ignites the circuit between the individual and the mass and thereby alters history.

It may alter history for better or for worse. Leaders have been responsible for the most extravagant follies and most monstrous crimes that have beset suffering humanity. They have also been vital in such gains as humanity has made in individual freedom, religious and racial tolerance, social justice, and respect for human rights.

There is no sure way to tell in advance who is going to lead for good and who for evil. But a glance at the gallery of men and women in *World Leaders—Past and Present* suggests some useful tests.

One test is this: Do leaders lead by force or by persuasion? By command or by consent? Through most of history leadership was exercised by the divine right of authority. The duty of followers was to defer and to obey. "Theirs not to reason why / Theirs but to do and die." On occasion, as with the so-called enlightened despots of the 18th century in Europe, absolutist leadership was animated by humane purposes. More often, absolutism nourished the passion for domination, land, gold, and conquest and resulted in tyranny.

The great revolution of modern times has been the revolution of equality. The idea that all people should be equal in their legal condition has undermined the old structure of authority, hierarchy, and deference. The revolution of equality has had two contrary effects on the nature of leadership. For equality, as Alexis de Tocqueville pointed out in his great study *Democracy in America*, might mean equality in servitude as well as equality in freedom.

"I know of only two methods of establishing equality in the political world," Tocqueville wrote. "Rights must be given to every citizen, or none at all to anyone . . . save one, who is the master of all." There was no middle ground "between the sovereignty of all and the absolute power of one man." In his astonishing prediction of 20th-century totalitarian dictatorship, Tocqueville explained how the revolution of equality could lead to the *"Führerprinzip"* and more terrible absolutism than the world had ever known.

But when rights are given to every citizen and the sovereignty of all is established, the problem of leadership takes a new form, becomes more exacting than ever before. It is easy to issue commands and enforce them by the rope and the stake, the concentration camp and the *gulag.* It is much harder to use argument and achievement to overcome opposition and win consent. The Founding Fathers of the United States understood the difficulty. They believed that history had given them the opportunity to decide, as Alexander Hamilton wrote in the first Federalist Paper, whether men are indeed capable of basing government on "reflection and choice, or whether they are forever destined to depend . . . on accident and force."

Government by reflection and choice called for a new style of leadership and a new quality of followership. It required leaders to be responsive to popular concerns, and it required followers to be active and informed participants in the process. Democracy does not eliminate emotion from politics; sometimes it fosters demagoguery; but it is confident that, as the greatest of democratic leaders put it, you cannot fool all of the people all of the time. It measures leadership by results and retires those who overreach or falter or fail.

It is true that in the long run despots are measured by results too. But they can postpone the day of judgment, sometimes indefinitely, and in the meantime they can do infinite harm. It is also true that democracy is no guarantee of virtue and intelligence in government, for the voice of the people is not necessarily the voice of God. But democracy, by assuring the right of opposition, offers built-in resistance to the evils inherent in absolutism. As the theologian Reinhold Niebuhr summed it up, "Man's capacity for justice makes democracy possible, but man's inclination to injustice makes democracy necessary."

A second test for leadership is the end for which power is sought. When leaders have as their goal the supremacy of a master race or the promotion of totalitarian revolution or the acquisition and exploitation of colonies or the protection of greed and privilege or the preservation of personal power, it is likely that their leadership will do little to advance the cause of humanity. When their goal is the abolition of slavery, the liberation of women, the enlargement of opportunity for the poor and powerless, the extension of equal rights to racial minorities, the defense of the freedoms of expression and opposition, it is likely that their leadership will increase the sum of human liberty and welfare.

Leaders have done great harm to the world. They have also conferred great benefits. You will find both sorts in this series. Even "good" leaders must be regarded with a certain wariness. Leaders are not demigods; they put on their trousers one leg after another just like ordinary mortals. No leader is infallible, and every leader needs to be reminded of this at regular intervals. Irreverence irritates leaders but is their salvation. Unquestioning submission corrupts leaders and demeans followers. Making a cult of a leader is always a mistake. Fortunately hero worship generates its own antidote. "Every hero," said Emerson, "becomes a bore at last."

The signal benefit the great leaders confer is to embolden the rest of us to live according to our own best selves, to be active, insistent, and resolute in affirming our own sense of things. For great leaders attest to the reality of human freedom against the supposed inevitabilities of history. And they attest to the wisdom and power that may lie within the most unlikely of us, which is why Abraham Lincoln remains the supreme example of great leadership. A great leader, said Emerson, exhibits new possibilities to all humanity. "We feed on genius. . . . Great men exist that there may be greater men."

Great leaders, in short, justify themselves by emancipating and empowering their followers. So humanity struggles to master its destiny, remembering with Alexis de Tocqueville: "It is true that around every man a fatal circle is traced beyond which he cannot pass; but within the wide verge of that circle he is powerful and free; as it is with man, so with communities."

1

Captain Moonlight and Captain Boycott

Captain Moonlight was abroad again in Ireland during the summer of 1880, and the acrid smoke from burning haystacks was in the night air. "Captain Moonlight" was a nickname for the agrarian secret societies of Ireland, most of whose members were Roman Catholic: the tenant and peasant defense associations; the men with blackened faces who roamed the countryside after dark, terrorizing the Protestant landlords and their collaborators. During the day, tenants who could no longer afford to pay the rent were summarily evicted from their meager holdings; during the nighttime hours, reprisals would follow: Haystacks belonging to landlords or their agents were set on fire, and their cattle were mutilated. Landlords and their employees were abducted from their homes and beaten, sometimes even executed.

They will do what we can make them do.
—PARNELL
speaking about the British government

Charles Stewart Parnell. Historian Robert Kee, writing about Parnell's methods of dealing with his British political adversaries, noted that Parnell's "principal tactic had been, from the first, one of breathtaking arrogance."

Parnell addresses an unruly antirent rally in the town of Limerick. The Protestant landlord was a masterful and often incendiary orator; huge crowds turned out for his public appearances.

In a country where only 12 percent of the population — the Protestant Anglo-Irish class — owned almost all of the land and controlled almost all of the wealth, and where the majority of the rest of the population — the Catholic tenant farmers — struggled to coax enough produce from their leased plots of land to eat and pay the rent, Captain Moonlight was an inevitable manifestation of a seemingly hopeless and endless cycle: the social and economic misery of the Catholics, calls for land reform and independence from England, and attempts by the British government to defuse the situation through a combination of legislation and police action. But this policy always failed in the long run, and even such an enlightened and progressive politician as British prime minister William Gladstone, who took office in 1868 with a promise "to pacify Ireland" and who did his best to keep that promise, could not solve what had come to be known as "the Irish problem." Inevitably the men of violence would come to the fore, the revolutionaries and saboteurs, the dynamiters and assassins, and the British government would be forced to resort to repression.

The summer of 1880, however, was different. What made it different was the presence of Member of Parliament Charles Stewart Parnell. Parnell was a most unlikely representative of Irish grievances; personally, he did not suffer under the yoke of British oppression, nor did he have to toil on the hard Irish earth for his own sustenance or face eviction when a wealthy Protestant landlord raised the rent beyond his means. In fact, Parnell himself was a moderately wealthy Protestant and a landlord. And yet the Irish Catholics trusted Parnell, seeming to recognize that he was a man who could deal with the British on their own terms and who could beat them at their own game. In the second volume of his history of Ireland, *The Green Flag*, Robert Kee asserts, "Never before had there been a man who thus deployed the essentially English qualities of inborn superiority and arrogance in the cause of the Irish peasant." And so, when Parnell spoke of justice and fair rent for the tenants and of home rule, or legislative independence, for Ireland, he brought a legitimacy and credibility to those causes that raised them to a new level. With Parnell as champion of the Irish, the British could no longer dismiss them as an uncivilized rabble incapable of governing themselves.

A victim of Captain Moonlight lies bleeding to death on a country road while his horse gallops away. Irish agrarian secret societies declared open season on landlords and their agents during the land wars of the late 19th century.

A despondent family of Irish Catholics, evicted from their home because they were unable to pay their rent. Such evictions were common in Ireland during Parnell's time, when failing potato harvests and impossibly high rents left tenant farmers and peasants homeless and destitute.

The peasants and small farmers turned out by the thousands to hear the Protestant landlord speak one September evening in 1880, at the town of Ennis, county Clare. The crowd was in an unruly, rebellious temper; the fires of agrarian unrest had been burning all summer, and a land agitation and rent-strike campaign orchestrated by the Irish National Land League (INLL) seemed to have the British government and the landlords on the defensive. There was a palpable atmosphere of insurrection in Ennis as Parnell mounted the platform in the town square.

He was impeccably dressed, a tall, slender, pale man with cold brown eyes and an aloof air. Eschewing the overblown rhetorical style that was popular with most politicians of his day, Parnell spoke in a clear, direct, unemotional manner. Addressing the issue of land grabbers, those tenants who took advantage of the misfortune of their neighbors by moving onto land from which one of them had been evicted, thus weakening the solidarity and effectiveness of the rent strike, Parnell posed a question to the crowd: "Now," he asked, "what are you to do to a tenant who bids for a farm from which his neighbor has been evicted?" Immediately answers were thrown up at Parnell from the seething mass: "Shoot him!" "Kill him!" The slightest of smiles played on Parnell's lips. "Now," he admonished, "I think I heard someone say 'shoot him,' but I wish to point out to you a very much better way, a more Christian and more charitable way, which will give the lost sinner an opportunity of repenting." Parnell waited for the crowd to grow completely silent, and then he continued: "When a man takes a farm from which another has been evicted you must show him on the roadside when you meet him, you must show him in the streets of the town, you must show him

A wealthy landlord leaves his family and estate under the protection of armed guards while he goes off to attend to business. During the land agitations, landlords, their families, and their property were under the constant threat of terrorism by tenant-defense associations.

After his workers refused to harvest his crops because of his harsh eviction policies, Captain Charles Boycott of county Mayo was forced to use the members of his own family as agricultural laborers until British troops arrived to lend a hand.

in the fair and in the market-place and even in the house of worship by leaving him alone. By putting him into a moral Coventry [a state of ostracism or exclusion], by isolating him from his kind as if he were a leper of old, you must show him your detestation of the crime he has committed, and you may depend on it that there will be no man so full of avarice, so lost to shame, as to dare the public opinion of all right-thinking men and to transgress your unwritten code of laws." Parnell paused for a moment to let his words sink in, but when he tried to continue his speech he could not — the roar of the crowd drowned out his voice.

Parnell's followers did not wait long to put to use the lesson on moral force he had given them at Ennis. The first and most famous victim of the new tactic of community ostracism was a landlord's agent for an estate in county Mayo. The agent was

well known for his high rents and eviction policies, and when harvesttime came, his farm laborers suddenly refused to touch his crops. His servants deserted him, merchants and tradesmen would not deal with him, bartenders would not serve him, and even the postmen were warned not to deliver his mail. The agent, fearing for his safety, fled to the city of Dublin, Ireland's capital, but when he tried to check into a hotel there he was denied lodgings by the Catholic proprietor. At this point the unfortunate gentleman decided to leave Ireland altogether, and he immediately set sail for England. His name, however, had already begun to be associated with that economic, social, and moral isolation to which he had been condemned. It would continue to be associated with that particular form of ostracism down through history. The land agent's name was Captain Charles Boycott.

2

Subjugation and Starvation

The recorded history of the country whose affairs Charles Stewart Parnell would dominate for more than a decade during the late 19th century began in the 5th century A.D., when an English-born Catholic bishop named Patrick, whom the Irish later adopted as their patron saint, traveled to Ireland to convert its people, who spoke a language called Gaelic, to Christianity. When the Dark Ages enveloped Europe at the end of the 5th century, Ireland, under the auspices of the Catholic church, kept the light of learning and civilization burning, becoming an important refuge for Christian scholars seeking to escape the political and cultural barbarism that had overrun the Continent.

Toward the end of the 12th century, King Henry II of England, hungry for new territory, invaded and occupied much of Ireland. England maintained a precarious hold on the country until the 16th century, but this situation changed during the period of religious and political upheaval known as the Reformation, which brought into existence a new variant of Christianity known as Protestantism. The Protestants rejected the authority of the pope — the head of the Roman Catholic church — and disagreed

> *Were not the people of Ireland born as free as those of England?*
> —JONATHAN SWIFT
> Irish satirist

Unlike most Irish nationalists, who were usually Catholic descendants of the original Gaelic inhabitants of Ireland, Charles Stewart Parnell was a Protestant from a wealthy landowning family of county Wicklow. From the beginning, however, his sympathies lay with the downtrodden Irish Catholics.

The patron saint of Ireland, St. Patrick. This Roman Catholic missionary from Britain converted the Gaelic natives to Christianity. According to a popular Catholic myth, St. Patrick used his holy staff to drive all the snakes of Ireland into the sea.

with Roman Catholics on several key issues of theology. In 1534, on the orders of King Henry VIII of England, the English Parliament renounced the pope's authority and established the Church of England, a Protestant institution that became England's official church. The Church of England's counterpart in Ireland was known as the Church of Ireland. In 1537, the Irish Parliament, in Dublin, was pressured by England into declaring Henry VIII "the Supreme Head of the Church of Ireland," and by 1541 Henry had been declared "King of Ireland."

Following her accession to the throne in 1558, England's Queen Elizabeth I confronted a series of rebellions by those Irish Catholics who had rejected the Reformation and the authority of the British Crown. Between 1556 and 1601, the English crushed four major Irish uprisings. Many of the English military commanders in Ireland who participated in putting down these insurrections were rewarded with grants of land seized from rebel landowners, thus beginning the *plantation*, or settlement, of large areas of the country by Protestants.

In the wake of the English conquest, Ireland's Catholics suffered increasingly severe social and economic deprivation. In the province of Ulster in northern Ireland — the other Irish provinces are Leinster, Munster, and Connaught — the government made so much land available to Protestant English and Scottish settlers that they became almost as numerous as native Catholics in the region. In time, Protestants would form a majority in six of Ulster's nine counties.

Further repression of the Irish commenced in 1649, at the end of the English Civil War, in which the Parliamentarian forces, led by an outstanding soldier and minor landowner named Oliver Cromwell, defeated the Royalist armies of King Charles I. Cromwell and many of his supporters were Puritans, which meant that their Protestantism and anti-Catholicism were particularly zealous, and they had been bitterly opposed to Charles I's pro-Catholic foreign policy. In 1649, when the war in England ended, the victorious Cromwell decided first to send a military expedition against the native Irish Catholics and the Old English (Anglo-Irish landowners who had remained faithful to Catholicism) and then forcibly to rearrange the Irish system of landownership so as to consolidate England's supremacy over Ireland.

The English ejected all the Irish Catholic landowners from all the good land in Ireland. In the country's most fertile areas, east of the Shannon River, the estates of Irish Catholic landowners who had participated in uprisings were expropriated and given to Protestant settlers. Those Catholic landowners who had not rebelled were "compensated" with confiscated rebel estates in western Ireland, mainly in the Province of Connaught, where the soil was extremely poor.

The Cromwellian settlement was one of the most traumatic events in Irish history. In 1641, Catholics had owned about 60 percent of the land in Ireland; by 1665, only 20 percent of the country's land was still in Catholic hands.

England's queen Elizabeth I reigned from 1558 to 1603, during which time she crushed several Catholic rebellions in Ireland. According to historian William Lecky, "the slaughter of Irishmen was looked upon" by members of the English aristocracy "as literally the slaughter of wild beasts."

Lord Protector of England Oliver Cromwell, with a wounded right arm, leads a charge of Parliamentarians against Royalist forces at the Battle of Marston Moor, Yorkshire, England in 1644. Following the English Civil War, Cromwell led an invasion force into Ireland and brutally subdued the rebellious Irish.

As the years passed, the situation continued to deteriorate. Most of the remaining Catholic landowners were dispossessed and their property given to Protestants. Under the terms of the English-legislated statutes known as the Penal Laws, Irish Catholics became second-class citizens in their own country. No Irish Catholic could become a member of Parliament (M.P.), practice law, vote in parliamentary elections, receive a university education, or serve in the Royal Navy. Most Catholics eked out a meager existence by farming tiny plots of land rented from wealthy Protestant landlords.

During the 18th century, Irish nationalism, once exclusively the preserve of the country's Catholics, began to permeate certain sectors of Protestant society. Some Protestants began to consider themselves more Irish than English. Two opposing camps formed in Irish Protestant politics: the court faction, which did not object to the London Parliament's control of the Irish Parliament; and the patriots of the country faction, who, while recognizing the ultimate authority of the Crown, wanted more autonomy for Ireland and a relaxation of the harsh Penal Laws. The leader of the patriots was a landowner and lawyer named Henry Grattan.

In 1782, the British agreed to the patriots' demands: The Dublin Parliament became an independent legislature under the British Crown. However, Grattan's Parliament, as the independent legislature was known, was corrupt and unrepresentative. Catholics, who composed 70 percent of the population, still could not vote.

In 1793, the revolutionary republican government that had been established in France following the overthrow of the monarchy in 1789 declared war on Britain. The British government, fearing that the radicalism that had swept France would find imitators among Ireland's nationalists, forced the Dublin Parliament to give the vote to Catholics — but only those who owned property valued at 40 shillings or more. The majority of Catholics — the peasants and tenant farmers — remained oppressed, poverty stricken, and disenfranchised.

Grattan's Parliament convenes in Dublin Castle, Dublin, Ireland, in 1790. The 500-year-old Irish Parliament was dissolved when the Act of Union was passed in 1801. Parnell's great-grandfather, Sir John Parnell, was a member of Grattan's Parliament, the last independent Irish Parliament before the union.

British statesman William Pitt became prime minister of Great Britain in 1793. Pitt, who believed that Ireland was "like a ship on fire" and that it had to be either "extinguished or set adrift," was largely responsible for the passing of the Act of Union between England and Ireland in 1800.

In 1800, British prime minister William Pitt decided that the only way to stop the unrest that still threatened to engulf Ireland would be to effect the legislative union of Britain and Ireland and then to bring about Catholic emancipation — that is, give Catholics the right to sit in the British Parliament at Westminster, in London. Accordingly, Pitt ordered Grattan's Parliament dissolved, and on January 1, 1801, the United Kingdom of Great Britain and Ireland came into existence. Pitt's subsequent efforts to secure Catholic emancipation failed, however. King George III refused to assent to it, and Pitt resigned. Catholic Ireland's prospects were not to improve again until 1823, when an Irish Catholic landowner and lawyer named Daniel O'Connell founded the Catholic Association, an organization committed to securing Catholic emancipation by constitutional means. O'Connell's organization rapidly grew into one of the most effective political mass movements in Irish history, and in 1828, British prime minister Lord Wellington, convinced that the continued withholding of Catholic emancipation would lead to civil war in Ireland, drew up the Catholic Relief Act, which became law in 1829. Catholics now had the right to sit in Parliament at Westminster.

In 1845, the Irish potato crop was partially ruined by blight. This development spelled disaster because potatoes were essential to the Catholic peasants' diet. Reports of starvation soon began to emanate from western Ireland, where, due to extensive subdivision of land and rural overcrowding, most farming was conducted on a subsistence basis. In 1846, when the potato crop failed completely, Ireland found itself confronted with the greatest disaster in its history. Peasants died by the thousands, and by 1848, when the potato crop failed yet again, Ireland was in a state of utter devastation. About 1 million Irish died in the famine, and 1 million emigrated, mainly to the United States. Mass emigration continued after the famine, and in 1855 it was estimated that some 2 million people had fled the country during the previous decade.

For the Irish, the trauma of the great famine was compounded by the failure of the British government to take action to deal with it. The Irish people's resentment of British indifference to their suffering, already considerable prior to the famine, increased dramatically in its wake.

By 1870, a famine-hardened Irish nationalism had developed into two main trends: the militant revolutionary movement of the Irish Republican Brotherhood (IRB) — more commonly known as the Fenians — which advocated the use of violence against the British; and the constitutional movement represented in Parliament by the Home Rule party, which sought to achieve Irish self-determination by bringing moral and political force into play against the British government. It was at this crucial juncture in Irish history that Charles Stewart Parnell made his entry into the political arena, but the story of this remarkable man begins in 1846, on an estate in county Wicklow.

Catholics attend an open-air mass in 19th-century Ireland. Despite the repressive policies of the British government, Roman Catholicism continued to flourish in Ireland; the Catholic priests also served as the guardians of Gaelic culture.

Charles Stewart Parnell was born on June 27, 1846, in the manor house of the Parnell family's Avondale estate, near Rathdrum, county Wicklow. His father, John Henry Parnell, was a relatively prosperous Protestant landowner who worked hard to improve the condition of his land and treated his tenants well. Charles's mother, Delia Tudor Stewart Parnell, was an intelligent and wealthy American socialite. John had met Delia while visiting the United States on business in 1834.

Although John and Delia Parnell had a large family — there were 11 children — their marriage was not a particularly happy one. After 1853, they were, for the most part, separated. Delia lived abroad most of the time, mainly in Paris and usually with some of the children in tow. Her husband stayed at Avondale.

Charles was an energetic and unruly child who, like most youngsters of his social class and background, was brought up through his early years by a succession of nannies. From the beginning he did not take kindly to discipline: One of his nannies once declared, "Master Charley is born to rule." In 1854, at age eight, Charles was sent to a boarding school for boys near Kirk Langley, England, but his disobedience soon resulted in his expulsion. His father decided that it would be best to have the headstrong boy educated by private tutors at Avondale.

In 1859, at the age of 49, John Parnell died of rheumatic fever. Charles then inherited Avondale, while the two other estates his father owned went to Charles's brothers, John Howard and Henry. After her husband's death, Delia began spending more time in Ireland and took a house in Dublin. In 1863, at his mother's insistence, Charles went back to England to cram for his university entrance examinations.

Parnell detested school. He found academic discipline no easier to bear than any other kind of discipline, and the only subjects he excelled in were mathematics and science, for which he had a natural flair. The combined efforts of the cram school's headmaster and a special tutor eventually produced the desired results, however, and in 1865 Parnell passed his entrance examinations and commenced his undergraduate studies, majoring in mathematics, at Cambridge University's Magdalene College.

Even though he made considerable progress in his studies, Parnell derived little satisfaction from his time at Cambridge. Most of the other students, who came from extremely wealthy backgrounds and had attended England's most fashionable private schools, either ignored those students they considered their social inferiors or behaved condescendingly toward them. Parnell also had to contend with the problem of English racial prejudice against the Irish, which in many instances made no distinction between the Catholic Irish and the Anglo-Irish. As a result, the young landlord's rebelliousness began to acquire focus and direction, and the cold and contemptuous attitude that Parnell would frequently display in his dealings with the English began to crystallize. In a conversation that he had with his brother John Howard during this period, Parnell commented, "These English despise us because we are Irish; but we must stand up to them. That's the way to treat the Englishman—stand up to him."

Parnell's mother, Delia Stewart Parnell, often indulged in anti-British rhetoric, but for her the subject of Irish nationalism was actually little more than a lively topic for conversation at social events.

Parnell's academic abilities were never put to the test of final examinations. One evening in May 1869, Parnell and a friend became involved in a street brawl with a local merchant. The merchant decided to press charges, and on May 21 the Cambridge County Court found for the plaintiff and fined Parnell a considerable amount of money. Five days later, the college authorities ordered Parnell to leave Magdalene and not to return until the next term began. Parnell, who considered both verdicts unfair, never went back.

From 1869 until 1875, Parnell remained preoccupied with managing Avondale, seemingly unconcerned with the political unrest that was once again brewing in Ireland. Although he was a patrician by instinct and breeding and liked to be shown the deference he considered his due, Parnell was also gifted with the ability — and the inclination — to associate without condescension with those who stood below him on the social scale, and unlike most other Protestant landlords, he enjoyed excellent relations with his Catholic tenants. Life at Avondale was good, and yet the young landlord was restless.

The Parnell mansion at the Avondale estate, in Rathdrum, county Wicklow. Parnell passed a happy early childhood at Avondale, and he never lost his love for the peaceful, rolling hills of the Wicklow countryside.

Parnell's younger sister Fanny was considered the most beautiful of the six Parnell girls. She was an ardent supporter of Irish nationalist causes, and as a girl she frequently became infatuated with the various Fenian heroes of her day.

While running his estate and participating in the constant round of banquets, formal dances, cricket matches, shoots, and hunting meets that were a major feature of Anglo-Irish rural life, Parnell began to make political connections with Ireland's nationalist elements, including the Home Rule League.

The Home Rule League, which was led by a Protestant lawyer named Isaac Butt, advocated "the inalienable right of the Irish to self-government." Butt was one of an increasing number of Protestants who believed that Protestants as well as Catholics had been victims of British racism and exploitation. By 1874, 60 of the 100 seats reserved for Irish M.P.s in the House of Commons — the lower house of Parliament — were held by supporters of the Home Rule League. (Approximately 40 of the 60 Irish M.P.s then sitting as Home Rulers were Liberals at heart and had aligned themselves with the Home Rule cause merely to enhance their prospects of election.)

Although most of the Home Rule League's leaders were initially skeptical about Parnell — all they knew about him was that he came from a distinguished Anglo-Irish family and that he could afford to pay his own election expenses — Butt was enthusiastic about the young landlord. He believed that the Home Rule party needed members of the Irish ruling class such as Parnell to deal more effectively with the two British parties — the Liberal party and the Conservative, or Tory, party — that were themselves dominated by members of the British ruling class, and he sensed that Parnell would prove an asset to the party.

An 1882 newspaper cartoon entitled "Going to the Ball in Troubled Times" humourously depicts the unnerving effects the political unrest of the period had on polite society in Ireland.

Isaac Butt was the founder and original chairman of the Home Rule party. Butt prided himself on being a gentleman, but the Parnellites in the Home Rule party eventually decided that Butt was too gentlemanly to be effective, and he was replaced as chairman by Parnell.

In March 1875 the Home Rule party ran Parnell as its candidate in a by-election in county Meath. Parnell's election campaign went extremely well, mainly because the local Catholic clergy, who enjoyed tremendous influence with the Catholic electorate, turned out in force to support him once it emerged that he believed that the government should abandon its policy of refusing to subsidize denominational education for Irish Catholics.

Parnell emerged victorious from the contest, and on April 22, 1875, he took his seat in the House of Commons. A few days later, in his maiden speech, he confronted the assembled members with a question: "Why," he asked, "should Ireland be treated as a geographical fragment of England?" He then declared that "Ireland is not a geographical fragment, but a nation." Taken together, Parnell's question and the answer he himself gave to it were a fitting prologue to a brilliant and tumultuous parliamentary career.

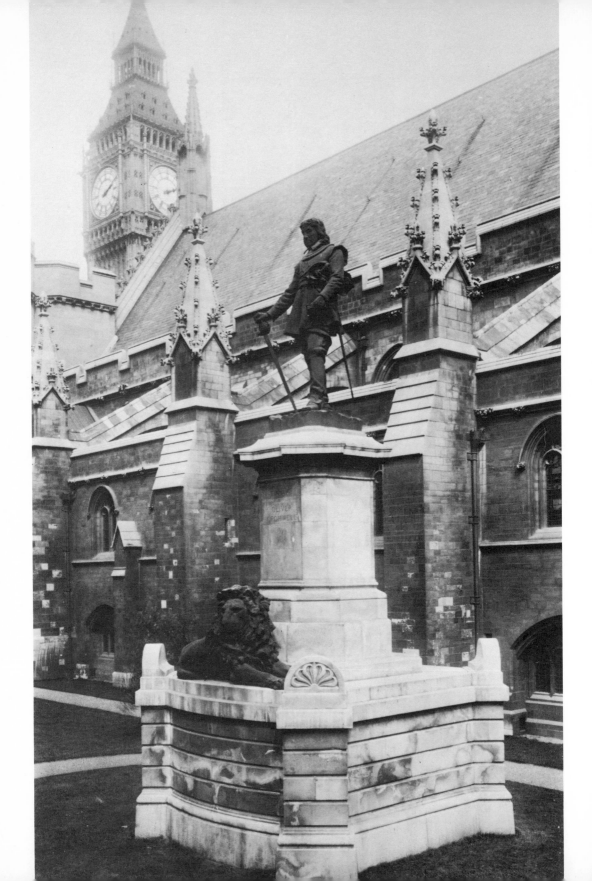

3

The Balancing Act

Parnell's arrival in the House of Commons coincided with the first use by an Irish M.P. of the parliamentary tactic of obstructionism. On April 22, 1875, Joseph Gillis Biggar, the hunchbacked and plainspoken pork merchant who was M.P. for Ireland's county Cavan, rose to make a point during a debate on "coercion," or repressive legislation, in Ireland. He then proceeded to speak for about four hours on the topic of swine fever. (According to the rules of the House of Commons, an M.P. could hold the floor for as long as he wanted to speak.) Biggar's calculated inaudibility and obvious determination to do nothing more than waste the House of Commons's time confounded all who heard him — except Parnell, who appreciated the value of obstructionism as a way to disrupt and manipulate parliamentary proceedings. Obstructionism would become one of the main weapons in Parnell's arsenal of parliamentary tactics.

We have got a splendid recruit, an historic name . . . young Parnell of Wicklow; and unless I am mistaken, the [English] will find him an ugly customer, though he is a good-looking fellow.
—ISAAC BUTT
chairman of the Home
Rule party

A statue of Oliver Cromwell stands guard over the Houses of Parliament in Westminster, London. When Parnell first took his seat in the House of Commons in 1875, Parliament was dominated by two parties — the Liberals and the Tories. Within five years, however, Parnell had transformed the Irish Home Rule party into a formidable parliamentary force.

Joseph Biggar, the hunchbacked Home Rule M.P. for county Cavan, introduced Parnell to obstructionism. According to Parnell biographer Joan Haslip, Biggar's main strategy in Parliament was to "make himself as disagreeable as possible."

Early in 1877, taking advantage of the broad knowledge of parliamentary procedure he had acquired during his first two years as an M.P., Parnell joined forces with Biggar. Biggar (who was also a member of the IRB at the time) and Parnell were an unlikely team, but they proved to be an extremely effective one. The two men and the handful of other Home Rule M.P.s who also advocated parliamentary activism initiated a campaign of obstruction that shook the House of Commons to its foundations. Their intent was to disrupt House of Commons business until the government addressed home rule issues to their satisfaction. Proceedings in the Commons occasionally ground to a halt, and newspapers in England and Ireland began running articles on the outrageous behavior of Parnell and the obstructionists.

On one occasion, Parnell so antagonized the vast majority of the British M.P.s that Isaac Butt, who felt that Parnell's behavior was "ungentlemanly," stepped in and reprimanded him before the entire assembly. Butt soon discovered, however, that in attacking Parnell he had damaged his own standing within the home rule movement at large. He had also made a formidable enemy. Parnell began criticizing Butt and his followers for their moderation in the pages of the *Freeman's Journal*, a leading Irish nationalist newspaper, and the dispute between the two men rapidly assumed critical proportions. In July 1877, Parnell, Biggar, and the obstructionists kept the House of Commons in continuous session for a total of 45 hours. In the process, they delayed the passage of important legislation concerning Britain's colonies in South Africa. Butt once again denounced the tactics of Parnell and the obstructionists, but the proud young landlord simply ignored him. In August, at the annual convention of the Home Rule Confederation of Great Britain (an organization that worked to build up the Irish vote in British constituencies), the delegates ousted Butt and elected Parnell president of the organization. Although Butt would retain his chairmanship of the Home Rule party itself, his authority had been permanently undermined.

By this time, several top members of the IRB had begun to consider Parnell the most distinctive and passionate figure in Irish nationalism's constitutional wing. Up to this point, the radical Fenians, who were committed to securing Irish independence by physical force, had despised those Irish nationalists — such as Isaac Butt — who believed that independence could be achieved through parliamentary action. But in August 1877, journalist and IRB member James J. O'Kelly, who worked with John Devoy, a leading member of the Clan na Gael (the IRB's American counterpart and major financial supporter), on the *New York Herald*, interviewed Parnell. The letter that O'Kelly then wrote Devoy contained an acute assessment of Parnell's position at the time and of the potential that Parnell had already begun to show in what was only the second year of his parliamentary career: "He has the idea," wrote O'Reilly, "that I held at the starting of the home rule organization — that is, the creation of a political link between the conservative and radical nationalists. . . . With the right kind of support behind him and a band of real nationalists in the house of commons, [Parnell] would so remold Irish opinion as to clear away many of the stumbling blocks in the way of progressive action." O'Kelly's observations failed to convince Devoy that the Home Rule party's leading obstructionist deserved the Clan na Gael's backing, but many Fenians in Ireland were beginning to take a view of Parnell that was similar to O'Kelly's.

In December 1877, Parnell traveled to county Mayo, one of the poorest counties in Connaught, to address a Home Rule League rally. The speech that Parnell made at the rally was important in two respects. First, he said that he might be willing to seek a greater degree of self-determination for Ireland than would be offered by home rule. Then he indicated that he now believed that the national question and the land question — the exploitation of Ireland's Catholic tenant farmers — could not justifiably be regarded as completely separate issues.

Parnell's contention that the land question and the national question were interrelated was both timely and original. During the previous three years

> *The only way to learn the rules of the House of Commons is by breaking them.*
> —PARNELL

In county Mayo, an Irish woman sits with her few belongings after being evicted from her home because she could not pay the rent. In 1880, more than 2,000 Irish Catholic families were evicted from their homes.

increased competition from American agriculture had caused a catastrophic drop in the prices Irish farmers received for their produce. Thousands of tenants had been forced to borrow from banks or moneylenders in order to make their rent payments, and by now most of them had exhausted their credit. Evictions soon followed, mainly in Connaught. The desperate situation that came to prevail throughout much of western Ireland was made even worse by widespread failure of the potato crop. Starvation reared its ugly head again, and the land question moved to the forefront of political debate.

By the end of 1878, Parnell's policy of using obstruction to force the British government to pay attention to Irish issues had finally persuaded Devoy that the Fenians would have much to gain from a working relationship with the Home Rule party activists. In October, with the approval of several other leading members of the Clan na Gael, Devoy unveiled a series of policy recommendations.

Devoy proposed that the Clan na Gael support Parnell and his fellow activists if the latter would agree to abandon their commitment to the concept of federal home rule, making "a general declaration in favour of self-government" instead. (The Fenians believed that a federal system was too moderate because it would leave Britain in control of all of Ireland's imperial issues, such as foreign and defense policy.) Devoy also proposed that Parnell and his supporters conduct "a vigorous agitation of the land question," not only pushing for the extension of the tenants' rights under the law but also having as their ultimate aim the abolition of landlordism and the establishment of a "peasant proprietary" — the system under which farmers actually own the land they work. Devoy then outlined the form that Fenian support for the parliamentary activists would take. The Fenians would collaborate with the parliamentarians on an interim basis while remaining faithful to the orthodox Fenian aim of securing Irish independence by physical force, or force of arms. Fenians acting in the spirit of the proposed policy would, while remaining revolutionaries, emerge into the open and seek to make Irish nationalist opinion as a whole more radical and, therefore, more effective.

The Supreme Council of the IRB condemned the new initiative and refused to forward Devoy's proposals to Parnell. Devoy protested that he was only advocating collaboration with the constitutionalists, but to no avail: The Supreme Council suspected that he was trying to forge a formal alliance. However, many Fenians in Ireland now believed that the hard-line, orthodox Fenians were actually harming the nationalist cause by refusing to get involved with the activist wing of the constitutional movement. The neo-Fenians — those Fenians who considered the land question relevant to the national question and who were prepared to work with the constitutionalists — realized that the constitutionalists might prove capable of significantly raising the caliber and effectiveness of the nationalist movement.

In April 1879, the neo-Fenians intensified their efforts to establish a collaborative relationship with Parnell. Devoy and the one-armed Michael Davitt met with Parnell and asked if he would be prepared to support a campaign of agitation aimed at securing justice for Ireland's tenant farmers. A leading nationalist of working-class origins who had lost an arm in a Lancashire factory accident, Davitt had been released from prison in 1877 on a ticket-of-leave, or probation, after serving 7 years of a 15-year sentence for arms trafficking. Parnell listened to Davitt and Devoy's proposals but remained noncommittal. At this point in his career, Parnell still considered the parliamentary struggle more important than any other.

In May 1879, Isaac Butt died of complications arising from a stroke, and the Home Rule party elected William Shaw, a moderate, to act as provisional chairman of the party for the rest of the parliamentary session. Parnell, as the guiding light of what was still a comparatively small group of activists within the party, realized that he stood little chance of getting elected to the chairmanship himself; at the same time, he came to realize that his only hope of securing personal ascendancy over the party lay in achieving personal ascendancy over all of the various elements of the nationalist movement in Ireland.

Michael Davitt was a lifelong Irish revolutionary; when he was four years old his family had been evicted from their farm. After serving a seven-year prison term for smuggling arms to the Fenians, Davitt founded the Irish National Land League and asked Parnell to be the league's president.

An irate Irish mob chases a landlord's agent — a familiar occurrence during the land agitations. In 1881 there were more than 4,000 incidents of agrarian violence and terrorism; Prime Minister William Gladstone then attempted to suppress the lawlessness with a coercion act, suspending *habeas corpus* in Ireland.

In June 1879, having finally recognized that the kind of movement proposed by Davitt and Devoy might be an ideal vehicle for his own drive for political preeminence in Ireland, Parnell had a second meeting with the two men. Exercising his habitual caution, he did not rush to embrace their ideas. Parnell showed no interest in actually leading the agitation they hoped to initiate, nor did he agree to Devoy's request that "the public movement" should do nothing to discredit the Fenian ideal of "complete national independence to be secured by the eventual use of physical force." Parnell wanted to keep the physical force business at arm's length, but he was prepared to support a combination of the home rule and the land movements in order to save the farmers and promote the home rule cause.

On June 8, 1879, Parnell traveled to Westport, county Mayo, to address a meeting that had been called to promote tenant rights, although he knew that in so doing he was risking condemnation as a Fenian sympathizer by the Catholic clergy, who believed that the meeting had been organized by Fenians. (The Catholic clergy loathed the Fenians' advocacy of violence and especially their nonsectarianism.) The faithful turned up at the meeting in droves, however, and witnessed Parnell's delivery of what turned out to be the most powerful speech of the day.

First, Parnell encouraged the tenants to "keep a firm grip" on their holdings and to stand up to the landlords and force them to reduce rents when times were hard. He then discussed the relationship between the land question and the national question. He also said that a campaign to extend the rights of the tenants would not — as orthodox Fenian opinion held — dilute the popular desire for self-government but would make it even stronger. He ended his speech on a note that drew tremendous applause from the crowd: "I have always noticed," he declared, "that the breaking down of barriers between different classes has increased their self-respect and increased the spirit of nationality amongst our people. I am convinced that nothing would more effectually promote the cause of self-government for Ireland than the breaking down of those barriers. . . . If we had the farmers the owners of the soil tomorrow, we would not be long without getting an Irish parliament."

Many who heard Parnell at Westport read more into his words than Parnell himself had intended to convey. Parnell was a politician of a type all too rare at that time in Ireland — a social conservative with a conscience. The fact that he had begun to associate with a radical like Davitt, however, led to a perception, particularly in conservative circles, that Parnell, too, was a radical.

Parnell's primary aim in regard to the land question was to force the government to grant the tenants the concessions known as the "3 Fs" — fair rent; fixity of tenure, or a guarantee that no tenant who paid his rent could be evicted; and free sale, or the right of the tenant to sell his land if he wanted to. He also believed, unlike the Fenians, that the land question could be settled without Irish separation from Britain and within the framework of the British constitution. Then, once Ireland's landlords and peasants were no longer at each others' throat over rent, the landlords would be in a position to assume the leadership of a united home rule movement, bringing to bear against the British government the full weight not only of their political preeminence but also of their *social* preeminence. The latter consideration was a particularly important element of Parnell's vision: He believed that a Home Rule party dominated by landlords would find it easier to deal with the British political parties — most of whose parliamentary representatives were themselves men of property — than would a Home Rule party dominated by tenant farmers whom the British M.P.s would consider their social inferiors.

The land agitation in which Parnell now became involved first assumed institutional form in August 1879, when Davitt founded the Land League of Mayo. The ultimate aim of this organization, whose manifesto stated that "the land of Ireland belongs to the people of Ireland," was to establish a peasant proprietary in place of the landlord system. Its leaders' more immediate concerns were of a less visionary and entirely more practical nature, however. Davitt and his colleagues wanted the organization

> *Unless we unite all shades of political opinions of the country, I fail to see how we can expect ever to attain national independence.*
> —PARNELL

to act as a pressure group for the defense and extension of tenant rights, preventing evictions and putting an end to *rack-renting*—the landlords' practice of raising the rent to a level the tenants could not possibly afford and then evicting the tenants for nonpayment. The organization would also hire lawyers to defend tenants in court when necessary; its methods would be nonviolent and legal.

The Land League of Mayo rapidly emerged as a highly effective organization. Davitt, encouraged by the league's success, considered the possibility of establishing an organization that would initiate and oversee a nationwide land agitation. In September 1879, convinced that Parnell's influence and prestige would make him the most effective leader of such an organization, Davitt discussed his idea with him. The Wicklow landlord informed the working-class agitator that he would, indeed, be willing

Parnell (seated at the head of the table) presides over a meeting of the Land League committee. The league supported both rent strikes and boycotts and advocated the redistribution of the land among the tenants. The Land League's slogan was, Rent at the Point of the Bayonet.

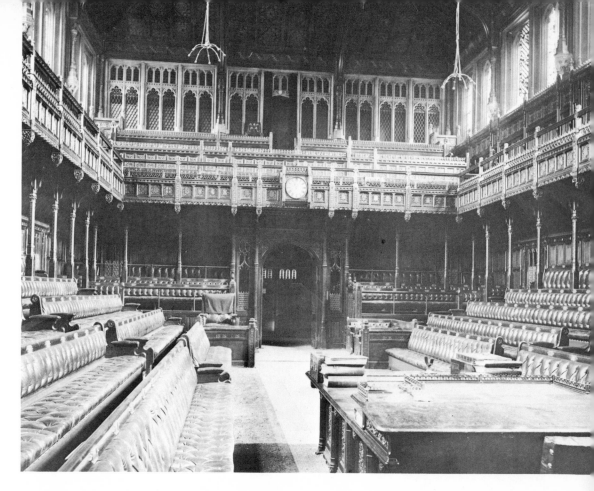

to serve as president of a national land league provided that its program was not as radical as that of the Land League of Mayo. A radical program, Parnell felt, would antagonize the British parties and compromise his own credibility and effectiveness in Parliament.

Davitt accepted Parnell's demand for a moderate program, and in October 1879, at a meeting held in Dublin's Imperial Hotel, the Irish National Land League was established, with Parnell as its president. The INLL's objectives were to "bring about a reduction in rack rents" and to facilitate "the obtaining of the ownership of the soil by the occupiers."

A link with the Fenians had been established, and Parnell was now the leader of what would become an immensely powerful mass movement. The stage was now set for one of the most tumultuous upsurges of nationalism in Irish history.

The chambers of the House of Commons, where Parnell waged his constitutional war against British misrule in Ireland, while his radical associates pursued a more extreme course. "There is force enough in moral power," Parnell avowed, "when it is brought to the support of a just cause."

4

The Language of Insurrection

In December 1879, Parnell traveled to North America to conduct a speaking tour to raise funds for the INLL. The tour, during which Parnell addressed Irish audiences in 60 cities in the United States and Canada, proved a great success, bringing in a considerable amount of cash for the INLL and a good deal more for famine relief.

When Parnell returned to Ireland in March 1880, a general election had been called for the following month, and the young INLL president immediately began campaigning for those among his own supporters who were standing as parliamentary candidates. The Liberals won a considerable majority in the election, taking 353 seats to the Conservatives' 238 and the Home Rule party's 61. At that time, the Home Rule party itself comprised three distinct factions. The Parnellites, as those Home Rule M.P.s active in obstructionism or involved in the INLL were known, numbered 24. The Whig faction, whose members inclined toward the Liberals and disapproved of Irish nationalism's more extreme manifestations — including the Parnellites —

Here's five dollars for bread and twenty for lead.

—an Irish immigrant in Troy, New York, on presenting a contribution to Parnell during his 1879 fund-raising tour of the United States

By 1880, Parnell had become the most hated man in England and the most popular man in Ireland. On May 17 of that year he was elected chairman of the Home Rule party, and journalists began referring to its members as "Parnellites."

In Dublin harbor, an illegal arms shipment, intended for Fenian use, is discovered and confiscated. Much of the funding for Fenian arms and supplies came from American members of the Clan na Gael, an organization devoted to Irish independence.

numbered 21. The remaining 16 Home Rulers held aloof from both other factions but had no distinct philosophy of their own. As the Parnellites became increasingly influential, however, the philosophy of their leader and the cardinal principles of the home rule movement itself became more closely identified.

On May 17, 1880, the Home Rule party met to elect a chairman for the forthcoming parliamentary session. Only 41 M.P.s attended the meeting, and of those 41, 23 voted for Parnell, 18 for William Shaw. Parnell's victory was a landmark in home rule politics. Most of the 20 Home Rule M.P.s who remained neutral in the election would eventually align themselves with Parnell. Twelve of the Whigs would formally secede from the party in January 1881. Thus, after May 1880 the Parnellite group essentially became the Home Rule party, which, during the decade that Parnell spent at its helm, would become the most effective parliamentary party in the history of preindependence Irish politics.

It was at the eve-of-session meeting that Parnell first met Captain William Henry O'Shea, Home Rule M.P. for a constituency in county Clare. O'Shea, although his political inclinations marked him as a Whig, voted for Parnell in the chairmanship election. A former army officer who owned a small estate in Ireland and also had an income from investments in banking and mining concerns owned by his family, O'Shea was an opportunist of the first order. Having failed to make a success of anything prior to his entry into politics, he had decided to associate himself with the rising star of Irish nationalism in order to advance his own career.

Parnell did not particularly care for O'Shea, and during the early part of the summer of 1880 he ignored the captain's invitations to dinner. This situation changed, however, one afternoon in July, when an invitation to dine at O'Shea's London apartment was delivered to Parnell by Katharine O'-Shea, Captain O'Shea's wife. A pretty and spirited woman who had borne her husband three children, Katharine was immediately attracted to the hand-

A terrorist bomb explodes under London Bridge in 1884, the year the militant Irish Fenians brought their nationalist struggle to London in the form of an extensive dynamite campaign. IRB bombers planted explosives in the House of Commons, Scotland Yard, and Westminster Abbey as well.

Katharine ("Kitty") O'Shea, wife of the handsome but unprincipled Captain William O'Shea, first met Parnell in the summer of 1880 and initiated the love affair that would last until Parnell's death.

some and charismatic Parnell. Her marriage to Captain O'Shea was not a happy one, and she and her husband had been effectively separated for several years. To maintain appearances, Katharine occasionally acted as hostess at her husband's dinner parties.

Largely because her husband was a hopeless businessman, Katharine and O'Shea were being supported by Katharine's extremely wealthy aunt, Mrs. Benjamin Wood, who, recognizing her niece's predicament but not wanting her to get divorced, had provided Katharine with an allowance and a well-appointed house in a small town a few miles south of London. Mrs. Wood had also provided Captain O'Shea with an allowance and an apartment in London. By the early fall of 1880, Katharine's feelings for Parnell were being reciprocated. Before the year ended, Katharine had become Parnell's mistress.

Meanwhile, Parnell and his party forged ahead with their endeavors to force the British government to adopt a constructive approach toward Irish affairs. Early in the 1880 parliamentary session, John O'Connor Power, a former member of the IRB Supreme Council who was now Home Rule M.P. for county Mayo, introduced legislation aimed at providing compensation for evicted tenants. In June, the chief secretary for Ireland, William Forster, introduced a bill on behalf of the government that partially satisfied the demands implied in O'Connor Power's proposals. That the government had introduced legislation of its own in response to a single Irish M.P.'s proposals greatly encouraged Parnell. He and his colleagues became enraged, however, when two months later the House of Lords (the upper house of Parliament) rejected the government's bill, which the House of Commons had approved.

The House of Lords' rejection of the bill inflamed anti-British sentiment throughout Ireland, and incidents of agrarian violence — in official terminology, "outrages" — became increasingly frequent. Angry tenants burned their landlords' haystacks and took potshots at their landlords' agents. Tenant-defense activists began accosting and beating up land grabbers. In September 1880, Parnell dramatically increased the moral force of the land agitation by urging its supporters to employ the method of nonviolent protest that later became known as boycotting. This radical new tactic soon proved effective. Whereas in the first 9 months of 1880 there were 2,110 evictions, the final quarter of the same year saw a mere 198 tenants ejected from their holdings. At the same time, however, despite Parnell's repeated denunciations of violence, outrages increased.

As the land agitation intensified, Forster and the lord lieutenant of Ireland, Francis Thomas de Grey Cowper, became determined to break the INLL. At the end of October, the government announced its intention to prosecute Parnell, Biggar, Home Rule M.P. and Fenian sympathizer John Dillon, Home Rule M.P.s Thomas Sexton and Thomas Daniel Sullivan, leading Fenian Patrick Egan, and another Fenian and land agitator named Thomas Brennan, along with several minor INLL officials, on charges of conspiring both to prevent the payment of rent and to poison tenant-landlord relations. The government's case against the defendants quickly came unstuck, however. In January 1881 the jurors declared the government's charges unsubstantiated. Shortly thereafter, the government suffered another setback in the form of further evidence that Parnell and his colleagues enjoyed broad popular support. The Parnell Defense Fund, established to defray the defendants' legal costs, rapidly received contributions totaling £21,000 sterling, which was then a very considerable sum of money. Parnell was delighted when he learned that 60 percent of the money had come from a subscription organized by the *Freeman's Journal* and that several leading Catholic churchmen had contributed to the fund. This meant that the INLL and the home rule movement now had on their side one of Ireland's most influential newspapers and a number of the country's most respected clerics.

In December 1880, Parnell moved to enhance party unity by ordering the party to put into practice the principle of *independent opposition*, one that dated back to the beginning of Butt's involvement in parliamentary politics but one the Home Rule party had rarely lived up to. At a meeting convened

William O'Shea was a political adventurer with no real convictions of his own. On first meeting O'Shea, Parnell was heard to comment, "That's just the kind of man we don't want in the party."

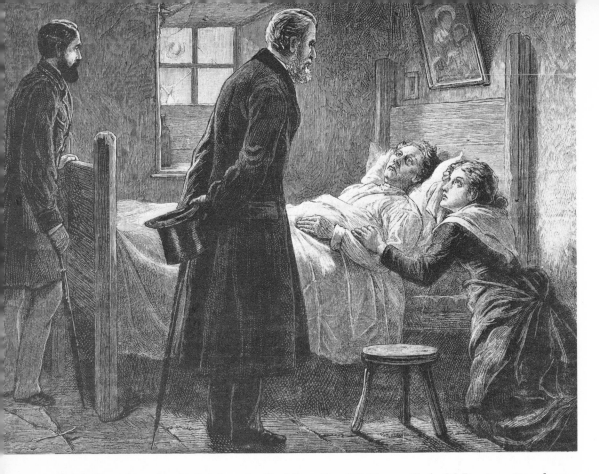

Chief Secretary for Ireland William Forster visits a victim of Captain Moonlight in the town of Tulla, county Clare. Forster, who was unfairly vilified in the nationalist press as a petty tyrant, was actually a devout Quaker who deplored violence.

in Dublin, the 38 Home Rule M.P.s in attendance voted, at Parnell's instigation, that in the House of Commons all the Home Rule M.P.s should sit on the opposition benches — that is, on the benches traditionally occupied by whichever of the two major British parties was out of power (At this time, the Conservatives were out of power). As Parnell had intended, this decision put the Whigs of the Home Rule party — who favored the Liberals — in a quandary: They would either have to side with the Parnellites and sit with the Conservatives or dissociate themselves from the Parnellites to remain loyal to the Liberals. As a result, a few weeks later Shaw and 11 other Whigs formally resigned from the party. A majority of the rest of the Whigs then agreed to sit with the activists, and the Home Rule party itself became still more closely identified with the Parnellite faction. Parnell was one step closer to establishing himself as the undisputed leader of a disciplined and effective parliamentary machine.

In January 1881, the government launched another offensive against the ongoing land agitation. Forster's introduction of the coercive Protection of Person and Property (Ireland) Bill, which proposed the suspension of ordinary law in any part of the country where the lord lieutenant thought it necessary, prompted an immediate campaign of obstruction by the Home Rulers. On February 3, in the House of Commons, the government responded by announcing that it had canceled Davitt's ticket-of-leave. This meant that Davitt, whose health had suffered badly during his previous incarceration, would be sent back to prison. Within minutes of the announcement, Dillon struck the first counterblow for the Home Rulers, deliberately interrupting a speech by British prime minister and Liberal party member William Gladstone. Dillon was immediately suspended from the House of Commons and forcibly ejected from the chamber. Parnell then jumped to his feet, launched into a bitter attack on the government, and was given the same treatment. The other Home Rulers followed suit, and by the end of

Parnell (seated in center with white top hat) and the members of his party practice the parliamentary tactic of independent opposition — sitting on the opposition bench and voting with the party that was currently the minority — in the House of Commons during a late session in 1880.

Parnell, followed by some of his colleagues, walks out of an uproarious House of Commons after being ejected for denouncing Prime Minister Gladstone, who had declared that Fenian Michael Davitt would be imprisoned again in retaliation for his INLL activities.

the evening 36 of them had been suspended and thrown out. This confrontation marked the beginning of a long and stormy association between the two men who would become the central players in the late 19th-century struggle over the issue of home rule: Gladstone and Parnell.

The suspension order against the Home Rulers was soon lifted. Having demonstrated that he and his followers were prepared to ride roughshod over the niceties of parliamentary procedure in response to any move by the government that they considered unreasonable, Parnell now proceeded to pursue a policy of combining radical form with moderate substance. While flirting with radicalism, Parnell kept the Home Rule party hard at work proposing revisions to a new land bill that Prime Minister Gladstone had introduced. The prime minister and his land-reform experts had designed the bill to concede the 3 Fs. Parnell and his colleagues were relatively happy with the bill as amended in the House of Commons, but the amendments that were then made to it in the House of Lords reduced it to little more than a complex attempt to control rent. The ever-pragmatic Parnell did not allow his reservations about the new legislation to blind him to its merits, however. Although Gladstone's bill neither applied to leaseholders nor did anything to alleviate the plight of tenants in the overcrowded areas of western Ireland, Parnell worked hard to ensure that the party's response to the bill would not impede its passage into law or destroy it altogether. That a handful of party members condemned the bill in its entirety did not disturb him. As long as a majority in the party maintained a constructive approach, he believed, occasional outbursts from enraged left-wingers would do no harm. Such outbursts, he felt, had a positive aspect in that they would keep the government on the defensive and the INLL suitably inspired.

Once the bill's passage was assured, Parnell moved to strengthen his control over the situation in Ireland. In July 1881, Egan, acting on Parnell's behalf, negotiated the purchase of three failing newspapers from their editor, a journalist named Richard Pigott. Parnell then merged them into a new publication, *United Ireland*, which would serve as his own mouthpiece and act as a counterweight to the editorial independence of the *Nation* and the *Freeman's Journal*.

Land League activists battle members of the Royal Irish Constabulary (RIC) during a confrontation at Belmullet, county Mayo. Prime Minister Gladstone blamed the rising tide of violence in the Irish countryside on Parnell and accused him of plotting the "dismemberment of the Empire."

In August, Parnell returned to Ireland. Later that month, Parliament passed the Land Law (Ireland) Act of 1881, which established a land court that would determine "fair rents" for tenants. Parnell, much to the annoyance of the government, immediately called on the INLL to bring test cases before the land court so as to ascertain the general position of the court's commissioners. He advised Ireland's tenant farmers to await the outcome of the test cases before deciding whether or not to take advantage of the land court. In September, the INLL's national convention endorsed Parnell's recommendations.

Infuriated by Parnell's attempts to undermine the new land legislation, Gladstone made a speech on October 7 at Leeds, England, in which he denounced Parnell as a "dangerous agitator" and an agent of "sheer lawlessness." On October 9, 1881, Parnell responded with the most inflammatory denunciation of the prime minister that he had yet delivered. On October 13 the government struck

Fenian and Home Rule M.P. John Dillon was one of Parnell's most valued lieutenants. He was arrested along with Parnell in October 1881 and imprisoned in Dublin's Kilmainham Jail, where he cowrote the No Rent Manifesto, which urged tenants to withhold rent from their landlords.

back: Forster had Parnell imprisoned in Dublin's Kilmainham Jail. The government's charge against Parnell was that he had attempted to prevent tenants from exercising their legal right to have their rent fixed under the provisions of the Land Law (Ireland) Act of 1881.

Gladstone and his colleagues imagined that by imprisoning Parnell they would strike a decisive blow against the INLL, the land agitation, and the nationalist movement at large. Events soon revealed, however, that imprisonment would be no barrier to Parnell's ongoing endeavors to expose the hollowness of Britain's claim to jurisdiction over Ireland. Parnell had, in fact, purposely provoked the government into arresting him. He had come to realize that the INLL was a spent force. Many of its members were failing to live up to its principles, frequently treating it as little more than a source of financing for lawsuits. Parnell dreaded incarceration because he would be cut off from his beloved Katharine. But Parnell recognized that his imprisonment would rally the entire Irish populace to his banner, and so, when Chief Detective Mallon of the Dublin police arrived at Parnell's hotel room on the morning of October 13 with a warrant for Parnell's arrest, Parnell dressed calmly and accompanied the officer without protesting.

Parnell arrives at Kilmainham Jail on the morning of October 18, 1881, having been arrested on the orders of Prime Minister Gladstone. Parnell was annoyed but undaunted by his arrest; referring to Gladstone, he promised from his Kilmainham cell that he would "live yet to trample on that old man's grave."

5

The Prisoner

Irishmen everywhere were outraged by the news of Parnell's imprisonment. The British crackdown on the INLL continued, and tensions were running high. During the week immediately following Parnell's arrest, the Royal Irish Constabulary (RIC) swooped down on several other leading nationalists and top INLL officials. By October 18, Parnell had been joined in Kilmainham by Dillon, Sexton, Brennan, *United Ireland* editor William O'Brien, acting secretary of the INLL J. P. Quinn, INLL official Andrew Kettle, and O'Kelly, who was now a Home Rule M.P. That same day, the prisoners issued a manifesto urging the tenants to "pay *no rents* under any circumstances to their landlords until the government relinquishes the existing system of terrorism and restores the constitutional rights of the people."

Before this wrong all other wrongs do grow pale, for they have clapped the pride of Erin's isle into cold Kilmainham Jail.
—Irish ballad about the jailing of Parnell

Charles Stewart Parnell was on the verge of becoming a national hero in Ireland in 1881. Gladstone had hoped to break the back of the land agitation by imprisoning Parnell. Instead, the seizure of Parnell made him a living martyr to the Irish cause, and the popularity of the Chief, as the people now called him, reached new heights.

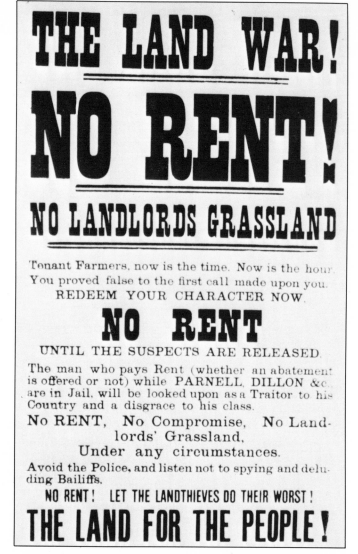

The no rent manifesto was issued from Kilmainham Jail
by the INLL men on October
18, 1881. Parnell signed the
manifesto despite his belief
that it would incite a new
wave of violence in the
countryside.

Parnell had grave reservations about the manifesto, but he signed it anyway, recognizing that his
endorsement of the manifesto would increase his
standing with the radical wings of both the INLL
and the home rule movement. The government responded to the no-rent manifesto within days of its
publication, declaring the INLL illegal and ordering
the organization's suppression. During the next few
weeks, the RIC arrested local INLL organizers in
towns and villages throughout the country.

The tenants, now leaderless, began, as Parnell realized they would, to flock to the land court. At the same time, outrages increased. Throughout the winter of 1881–82, the members of Ireland's numerous agrarian secret societies took to the hillsides and hedgerows once again, beating up or shooting land grabbers, policemen, and landlords' agents, maiming cattle, and setting fire to haystacks. In Kilmainham, Parnell reacted uneasily to reports of the explosion of anarchy. During its heyday, the INLL had usually managed, even in the face of extreme provocation by the government, to hold back the men of violence. Now, however, the organization's general deterioration meant that it could no longer perform the vital function of promoting the importance of moral force and self-discipline. Lawlessness and physical force had come to the fore in Ireland once again.

Under the watchful gaze of two guards, Parnell receives a visitor in his Kilmainham jail cell. For Parnell, conditions in Kilmainham were far from harsh; he spent most of his time reading, sleeping, or playing chess with fellow inmates.

Officers of the Royal Irish Constabulary discuss the day's activities. Originally known as the Irish Constabulary, the police force was rewarded with the title *Royal* for its dedicated pursuit of Fenian elements in Ireland.

Even though conditions in Kilmainham were not harsh, Parnell found his incarceration unbearable. He was especially concerned about the effect of his imprisonment on Katharine O'Shea, who was now pregnant with their first child. In November 1881, Katharine informed him in a letter that Captain O'Shea had stayed with her at Wonersh Lodge for a few days. Although much of the evidence concerning Captain and Mrs. O'Shea's relationship at this time is of a conflicting nature, some historians think it probable that they were still having physical relations. If this was the case, Parnell seems either not to have realized it or, if he did realize it, to have given no indication that he did. Writing in reply to Katharine's letter, Parnell declared that he found it "frightful that you should be exposed to such daily torture," never doubting that Katharine hated the time spent with her husband when actually she may have been enjoying it. The strongest evidence that Katharine may have been misleading Parnell about her fidelity to him at this time is that Parnell and Captain O'Shea each believed Claude Sophie — the daughter to whom Katharine gave birth in February 1882 and who died at the end of April 1882 — to be his own.

In April 1882, Parnell was released on parole so that he could attend a nephew's funeral in Paris. Following his arrival in London en route to the French capital, Parnell met with Captain O'Shea, who then acted as an intermediary between Parnell and Gladstone. O'Shea informed the prime minister, in writing, that agrarian terrorism and the Home Rule party's opposition to the impending implementation of changes in parliamentary procedure designed to prevent obstructionism would abate if the government agreed to do two things: extend the provisions of the Land Law (Ireland) Act of 1881 to include leaseholders and tenants in arrears (fallen behind) with their rent and establish a commission to investigate the plight of Ireland's agricultural laborers. At the same time, and in this instance *without* Parnell's authorization, O'Shea wrote to Joseph Chamberlain, the brilliant young president of the Board of Trade and leader of the Radical, or left-progressive, wing of the Liberal party. O'Shea informed Chamberlain that a Liberal compromise "might be met by the most influential Irishman of the day [Parnell] in a candid and moderate spirit."

O'Shea's overtures persuaded the government that it would be wise to give the imprisoned nationalist leaders a positive response — while noting a determination to make no major alterations to existing policy until the violence in Ireland subsided. On April 22 the cabinet authorized Chamberlain to hold discussions with O'Shea and other Irish M.P.s to find out their opinions but not to negotiate with them. Later that same month, having again conferred with Parnell as the latter returned to Ireland from Paris via London, O'Shea visited Chamberlain and informed him that Parnell would publicly condemn agrarian terrorism and all other forms of intimidation if the government would — as Chamberlain's memorandum about the meeting puts it — "announce a satisfactory plan of dealing with arrears." On April 23, Parnell conferred with Justin McCarthy, the vice-chairman of the Home Rule party, who then informed Chamberlain that if the government took action to redress the

For Parnell, the most painful aspect of his imprisonment was separation from Katharine O'Shea, who was pregnant. Some historians believe that Parnell's release was secured by Katharine through her manipulation of her husband, Captain O'Shea.

Joseph Chamberlain, leader of the Radical, or left-progressive wing of the Liberal party, acted as spokesman for Gladstone's cabinet in the Kilmainham negotiations. Chamberlain favored Parnell's release after Parnell promised he would publicly condemn the escalating land agitation.

grievances of the Irish people, Parnell would secure the revocation of the no-rent manifesto and advise the tenants to settle with the landlords.

Parnell returned to Kilmainham on April 24. On April 25, the cabinet, most of whom now felt that Parnell, Dillon, and O'Kelly should be released in exchange for assurances that they would not oppose the introduction of temporary and selective coercive legislation, informed the nationalists' spokesmen that they would guarantee swift action to settle the arrears question if the Home Rule party would accept a government decision to reject a bill amending the Land Law (Ireland) Act of 1881, a bill that Home Rule M.P. John Redmond had recently introduced.

The Irish reaction was favorable. On April 29, however, O'Shea conferred with Parnell, who promptly decided to raise the stakes without consulting his fellow prisoners. In a letter addressed to O'Shea and dated April 28 to give the impression that he had written it prior to meeting with O'Shea, Parnell said that a settlement of the arrears question and the extension of the provisions of the Land Law (Ireland) Act of 1881 to cover leaseholders "would enable [the Home Rule party] to cooperate cordially for the future with the Liberal Party in forwarding Liberal principles and measures of general reform."

Parnell's proposals caused consternation among the leaders of the Liberal party. O'Shea, having arrived back in London on April 30, showed the letter to Forster, whose response was one of skepticism. Forster's misgivings turned to sheer astonishment when O'Shea then gave him a verbal summary of what he said were Parnell's thoughts on the current situation. What O'Shea said to Forster did not, in fact, reflect Parnell's true position. In a subsequent letter to Gladstone, the infuriated chief secretary for Ireland informed the prime minister that, according to O'Shea, Parnell had asserted that "the conspiracy which has been used to set up boycotting and outrages will now be used to put them down, and that there will be a union with the Liberal Party." Parnell was, in fact, in favor of using "extremists" — that is radical, physical force-oriented republicans — to put down the agitation, but he had not advocated union with the Liberals.

The idea of extremists being used to rein in the agitation horrified Forster, who was already heavily preoccupied with the suppression of extremism. Gladstone, however, having become convinced that Forster's inflexibility was as great an obstacle as extremism to the possibility of peaceful change in Ireland, found much that he liked in what he thought were Parnell's proposals. The prime minister announced that he now considered it safe to release Parnell, O'Kelly, and Dillon, because they appeared to be willing to take action to bring the land agitation to an end.

Irish National Land League members rally on a stormy night in county Kildare. During Parnell's incarceration the situation in the Irish countryside became increasingly volatile.

Parnell was now determined to put the entire nationalist movement on a new, constitutional footing, thus leaving the extremists stranded in a political wilderness. The land agitation had frightened the cabinet and convinced hundreds of thousands of Irish nationalists that in the agitation they had an effective means of realizing their hopes and aspirations, but Parnell believed that the agitation was now doing more harm than good.

On May 2, 1882, Parnell, O'Kelly, and Dillon were released from jail. Two days later, in protest, Forster resigned as chief secretary for Ireland. Gladstone then appointed Lord Frederick Cavendish to replace him. That same day, Sir William Harcourt, Gladstone's secretary of state for home affairs, horrified the Conservatives with an announcement that he had ordered Davitt's release from jail. Many Conservatives were now completely convinced — and would remain convinced — that the Liberals had struck a deal with Parnell, despite Parnell and Gladstone's protestations to the contrary.

The stage was now set for the opening moves of Parnell's new constitutional offensive. Unfortunately for Parnell and his followers, however, an unexpected intervention by frustrated extremists almost destroyed their credibility even as they adjusted to their newfound freedom.

"The Old Man," Prime Minister William Gladstone, agreed to the release of Parnell and his colleagues from Kilmainham despite the objections of Chief Secretary William Forster. Gladstone believed that only Parnell could successfully defuse the land war.

Lord Frederick Cavendish took over as chief secretary for Ireland after William Forster resigned in protest of Gladstone's decision to release Parnell and the other Land League representatives from prison.

On the evening of May 6, 1882, four days after Parnell's release from Kilmainham, Lord Frederick Cavendish and Undersecretary for Ireland Thomas Burke were stabbed to death with surgical knives as they walked together in Dublin's Phoenix Park. The perpetrators of this brutal crime were members of the Irish National Invincibles, a republican secret society. Horror swept across England. Parnell first learned of the crime from the headlines of the London *Observer*, and as he read he no doubt saw the work he had done to bring credibility to the Irish nationalist cause begin to vanish. He said to Katharine O'Shea, "I shall resign. I can't go on." His worst fears about the extremist elements of Irish nationalism had come true.

6

Machine Politics

Recognizing that the hideous crime in Phoenix Park would cause an upsurge of anti-Irish feeling throughout Britain and make it difficult for Gladstone to maintain his moderate policy on Ireland, Parnell immediately offered the prime minister his resignation. Gladstone, however, convinced that Parnell's departure from the House of Commons would hinder the Liberals' efforts to devise an Irish policy acceptable to the Irish themselves, managed to persuade Parnell not to resign. On May 7, Parnell made public his own feelings about the atrocity in Phoenix Park, appending his signature to Davitt, Dillon, and McCarthy's "manifesto to the people of Ireland," which condemned the murders. The next day, in the House of Commons, he vilified the assassins in a speech of unbridled fury, convincing a great many people of his absolute sincerity. Parnell's actions did not suffice, however, to dissuade the government from bringing in new coercive legislation. On May 11, Harcourt introduced the harsh Prevention of Crime (Ireland) Bill.

How can I go on if I am stabbed in the back this way?
—PARNELL
on learning of the Phoenix
Park murders

The industrial city of Belfast, home of Parnellite M.P. Joseph Biggar. The brutal murders in Phoenix Park elicited a general outcry of horror and condemnation from both the British and the Irish. Biggar, however, was a hardened revolutionary, and he saw no reason to mourn the deaths of two agents of British misrule.

THE MEN WHO WERE TRIED IN CONNECTION WITH THE MURDER, IN PHŒNIX PARK, DUBLIN, OF LORD FREDERICK CAVENDISH AND Mr. THOMAS HENRY BURKE.

Twelve of the 26 men who were tried and convicted in connection with the Phoenix Park murders in Dublin. They were all members of the Irish National Invincibles, a militant republican faction.

Parnell worked extraordinarily hard to persuade the government to moderate the provisions of the new coercion bill, hoping to prevent the passage of legislation that might provoke further outrages. In an attempt to influence the dispute that was then raging in the cabinet between Harcourt, who favored coercion, and Gladstone and Chamberlain, who favored conciliation, the Irish leader suggested that coercion be delayed until the enactment of the recently introduced Arrears Bill, which proposed that the state pay 50 percent of the money owed by tenants in arrears and compel the landlords to accept the cancelation of the remainder of the debt. But during the latter part of June 1882, it became increasingly apparent that the government intended to pass the Prevention of Crime (Ireland) Bill before passing the Arrears Act. Once again the secret societies stepped up their violent campaign. Meanwhile, in the House of Commons, the Parnellites' continuing obstruction campaign against the new coercive legislation did nothing to improve the cabinet's attitude. In July, Parliament passed the Prevention of Crime (Ireland) Act. In August, however, Parnell was able to claim victory when Parliament passed the Arrears Act, which contained many provisions that Parnell had insisted be included. As Parnell had predicted, the Arrears Act did more to calm agrarian unrest in Ireland than any amount of coercion: Of the 135,997 tenants who filed claims for state assistance in paying off their arrears under the new legislation, 129,952 had their claims allowed. Agrarian unrest immediately began to decline.

In September 1882, Parnell hosted a conference at Avondale to establish a new, open organization that would replace the INLL as the primary vehicle for the popular constitutional movement, an organization that would be much more conservative than the INLL and that he himself would direct and control. The founding convention of the new organization, which was known as the Irish National League (INL), took place in Dublin in October 1882.

Unlike previous Irish nationalist organizations, the INL was exclusively concerned with parliamentary objectives, dominated by parliamentarians, and committed to purely constitutional agitation. For Davitt and the radicals, Parnell's successful bid to make constitutionalism the cornerstone of Irish nationalism was a setback. Writing of the birth of the INL in *The Fall of Feudalism in Ireland: Or the Story of the Land League Revolution*, published in New York in 1904, Davitt asserted that "it was, in a sense, the overthrow of a movement and the enthronement of a man; the replacing of nationalism by Parnellism; the investing of the fortunes and guidance of the agitation, both for national self-government and land reform, in a leader's nominal dictatorship."

Sir William Harcourt, secretary of state for home affairs in the Liberal cabinet, had Parnell under the surveillance of private detectives and received regular reports on Parnell's activities — including his assignations with Katharine O'Shea.

Lord Randolph Churchill of the Conservative party twirls his mustache while a disgruntled Gladstone (seated on front bench on the right) studies parliamentary documents. Churchill's party came into power — and Gladstone's party fell out — when the Conservatives and Home Rulers voted together against the Liberals in June 1885.

Throughout 1883, the Chief, as Parnell had come to be known, tightened his hold on the INL's constituency organizations. During the same period, Parnell also worked hard to identify himself and his party ever more closely with Catholic interests. Recognizing that the party could not make decisive advances without the active support of a majority of the Irish Catholic clergy, he now began to dissociate himself from Chamberlain and the Radicals, who favored nondenominational education and believed that religion should be kept out of politics.

Parnell's determination to compensate for the loss of left-wing support by securing increased backing from the more conservative sectors of Irish society grew throughout 1884. The force with which he preached the conservative gospel was partly due to his misgivings about the possible outcome of the Reform (Franchise) Act, which was passed in June 1884. In Ireland, the new legislation expanded the electorate from 225,000 voters to 738,000. Most of the new voters were small farmers and agricultural laborers. Many Whigs and Conservatives hoped that the new voters would form a constituency in Irish politics that would counter the power of the middle-class farmers and professional men who constituted

Parnell's main support base. Parnell, for his part, saw that if he could convince the new electors that his policies were in their best interests, the Home Rule party would stand a good chance of returning more candidates at the next general election.

By promoting constitutionalism and conservative principles, Parnell eventually realized one of his chief ambitions: He gained the support of the most conservative, and perhaps the most influential, institution in all of Irish society — the Roman Catholic church. In October 1884 the Irish bishops agreed to entrust the Home Rule party with Irish Catholic educational interests. For Parnell and his colleagues, this was a major breakthrough. As Conor Cruise O'Brien notes in *Parnell and his Party, 1880–1890*, "Catholic interests in what is, from the religious point of view, the most important of political questions [education], were thus entrusted to a group which, less than five years before, the majority of bishops had regarded as dangerously subversive. Parnellism was now accepted; from now on in Catholic Ireland no one but a crank could condemn it as revolutionary."

Since the Phoenix Park murders, Gladstone had been sluggish in responding to Irish grievances; for the most part the Liberal majority simply ignored Irish issues whenever possible. Parnell decided it was time to put pressure on Gladstone: In May 1885, Parnell had his first meeting with Lord Randolph Churchill, a young and energetic member of the Conservative faction known as the Fourth party, which favored conciliation in Irish affairs and espoused a progressive form of conservatism called Tory democracy. Churchill told Parnell that if the Conservatives won the next general election and he himself received a cabinet post, he would oppose the renewal of coercion. Accordingly, on June 9, 1885, on Parnell's orders, the Home Rule party sided with the Conservatives in voting for a budget amendment of which the Liberals disapproved. The Liberal government lost by 12 votes, and subsequently on June 11, Gladstone and his colleagues resigned. The Conservatives then formed a government.

Lord Salisbury, the leader of the Conservative party, was responsible for passing some of the most progressive legislation concerning Ireland. The courtship between the Conservatives and the Home Rulers ended abruptly in January 1886, however, when the Parnellites helped the Liberals regain the majority in the House of Commons.

Upon coming to power, Conservative leader Lord Salisbury dropped coercion altogether. Weeks later the Conservatives made another major concession to the Irish, securing the passage of legislation that authorized giving state assistance to tenants to enable them to buy land. The passage of the Ashbourne Act — so named for its originator, Edward Gibson, First Baron Ashbourne—represented a considerable victory not just for the Home Rulers but for all Irishmen who had supported the INLL. For the first time, a British government had acknowledged that the ultimate solution to the land question in Ireland was the creation of a peasant proprietary.

The Chief forged ahead with his plans to convert the Home Rulers into a more monolithic party. Another important element of Parnell's drive to enforce discipline, unity, and loyalty in the party leadership was the introduction of a new party pledge. The new pledge read as follows: "I pledge myself that in the event of my election to parliament I will sit, act and vote with the Irish parliamentary party and if at a meeting of the party . . . it be decided by a resolution supported by a majority of the entire parliamentary party that I have not fulfilled the above pledge I hereby undertake forthwith to resign my seat." The unity and discipline of the Parnellite pledge evidenced how very far the party had come from the anarchy of Butt's day.

In October 1885, Parnell's preoccupation with the upcoming general election and the British parties' attitudes toward home rule suddenly found itself accompanied by an equally intense preoccupation with the attitudes of a single member of his own party — Captain O'Shea. O'Shea announced that he expected to be nominated as the Home Rule candidate for county Clare in the general election but that he would not take the party pledge. The county Clare INL organization promptly refused to accept O'Shea as a candidate. The captain, still determined to advance his career by continuing his association with Parnell, informed the Irish leader that if he did not secure an Irish seat in the House of Commons, he might find it impossible to keep silent any longer about Parnell's relationship with his wife.

Despite the anguish that O'Shea's blackmail was causing him, Parnell was able to view the overall outcome of the general election with great satisfaction. The Home Rule party had won 86 seats in the House of Commons. This number exactly equaled the majority the Liberals now enjoyed over the Conservatives: The former had won 335 seats; the latter, 249. Parnell and his lieutenants' rigid enforcement of party discipline, combined with their iron-fisted management of the INL convention system, had enabled Home Rule party candidates to win all but two of the 70 seats in Leinster, Munster, and Connaught. Even in predominantly Protestant Ulster, which contained 33 constituencies, the Home Rule party now had triumphed, and Parnell was in a position to make home rule the most important issue in British politics.

Following the general election, Salisbury formed a government. Parnell continued to probe both the Liberals and the Conservatives concerning the possibility of concessions on home rule. His activities on this front were conducted in parallel with the renewal of his endeavors to satisfy Captain O'Shea. Shortly after the general election, O'Shea had intimated to Parnell that he wanted to be adopted as the Home Rule candidate for a by-election in Galway City, Ireland. Parnell recognized that persuading the party and the Galway INL organization to back

Conferring in the lobby of the House of Commons are, from left to right, Chamberlain, Parnell, Gladstone, Churchill, and Salisbury. By 1886, the four British statesmen were painfully aware of the power Parnell commanded in Parliament.

O'Shea — who still refused to take the party pledge — would be extraordinarily difficult. The outcome of the general election had, after all, demonstrated the value of party discipline, and the pledge itself was a fundamental means of enforcing that discipline. Many party members, Parnell realized, might consider an attempt by their leader to force an unpledged candidate on the party absolutely inexplicable and possibly even inexcusable.

Throughout January 1886, Parnell mulled over his dilemma, keeping his thoughts to himself and coming to no conclusions. At the same time, recent developments on the wider political scene demanded much of his attention.

On December 17, Herbert Gladstone, William Gladstone's son, had informed three journalists who were interviewing him that his father, still very influential in British politics, was about to declare himself in favor of home rule. Few people found Gladstone's subsequent denials convincing; it was obvious that Gladstone was sending a signal to Parnell that he was now ready to address home rule. The Conservatives, on the other hand, were already considering renewing coercion in Ireland, and their rather uneasy association with the Home Rulers was beginning to falter. The balance of power between the Conservatives, the Liberals, and the Home Rulers shifted again on January 27, 1886, when the Conservative government was defeated in a vote on an amendment to a bill concerning agricultural policy. Salisbury immediately began making arrangements for the transfer of power to the Liberals.

Five days after the fall of Salisbury's government, preparations began for the Galway by-election. The local INL organization had already put forward a pledged candidate, Michael Lynch. Parnell continued to brood on the problem. Finally, on the evening of February 5, Parnell informed O'Connor that he intended to run O'Shea in Galway. Appalled, O'Connor asked Biggar to help him prevent Parnell from proceeding any further with his plan.

Biggar sided with O'Connor. Both men recognized that opposing Parnell and possibly provoking a split in the party when Gladstone seemed to be about to introduce a home rule bill would be dangerous, but they felt obliged nevertheless to oppose O'Shea's candidacy. The two men not only loathed O'Shea's politics but also suspected that O'Shea's wife was Parnell's mistress. The thought of Parnell helping O'Shea for reasons relating to his affair with O'Shea's wife was more than they could bear.

In the early hours of February 6, while Biggar and O'Connor were still en route to Dublin, Parnell sent Edmund Dwyer Gray, the editor of the *Freeman's Journal*, a misleading telegram that distorted the truth of the situation but had the desired effect of securing Gray's backing for O'Shea's candidacy. In the telegram, Parnell also informed Gray that he would resign as party leader if the party refused to accept O'Shea as its candidate.

When Biggar and O'Connor arrived in Dublin later that same morning, they discovered that the *Freeman's Journal* had already published O'Shea's election address. The two men, along with their chief ally, an influential Home Rule M.P. named Timothy Healy, quickly realized that should they now choose to continue to oppose O'Shea's candidacy, they would have to do so in public. As far as O'Connor was concerned, fighting Parnell on principle was one thing, but fighting him in public for any reason was quite another. He backed out of the dispute, recognizing that Parnell, by supporting O'Shea, had made the main issue his own leadership rather than O'Shea's election.

On February 10, Parnell arrived in Galway City. At the station, he found himself confronting a large and extremely hostile crowd of Lynch's supporters. Adopting an expression of disdain, Parnell ignored their jeers and strode into the station hotel. There, at a meeting held behind closed doors and attended only by M.P.s, he faced down a barrage of criticism from Healy, who reminded him that he had threatened to resign if O'Shea was not selected. Parnell promptly flattened Healy by making it plain that he did not intend to sacrifice his own position under any circumstances. "I have no intention," he said, "of resigning my position. I would not resign it if the people of Galway were to kick me through the streets today."

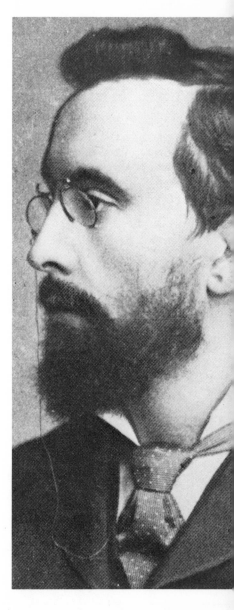

Timothy Healy was the secretary of the Home Rule party and Parnell's personal assistant. The young Healy idolized the Chief, but when he learned of Parnell's affair with Katharine, he turned on his leader and bitterly denounced him.

Parnell then went out to Lynch's supporters, who began heckling as soon as they saw him. Once again, Parnell faced them down. He then secured their undivided attention with a statement that guaranteed their allegiance — even though it was not strictly true. "When," Parnell asked, "was it so absolutely essential to uphold my authority as at this moment when I hold in my hand the measure that will secure peace and prosperity to this long neglected country?" The "measure" to which he referred was, of course, home rule. Sensing that his bluff had brought him close to victory, Parnell then said, "Reject Captain O'Shea, destroy me, and there will rise a shout from all the enemies of Ireland: 'Parnell is beaten, Ireland no longer has a leader.'" The Parnellites triumphed, and O'Shea, whom Parnell had ignored throughout his visit to Galway, won the by-election by a large majority.

Four months after the confrontation in Galway, O'Shea retired from politics. Though the ostensible reason for his leaving was his opposition to Gladstone's recently introduced Home Rule bill, the real reason had more to do with Parnell's involvement with his wife. Suggestions that the relationship between Parnell and the O'Sheas was less than reputable had begun to appear in the gossip columns.

Galway City's business district was the scene of the February 10, 1886, confrontation between Parnell and the supporters of Michael Lynch. Captain O'Shea had blackmailed Parnell into backing him, instead of Lynch, as the Home Rule candidate for Galway City, and Lynch's supporters were outraged.

By the beginning of 1887, Parnell was beginning to succumb to the pressures of having to conceal his relationship with Katharine O'Shea. He shaved off most of his beard and began to adopt a series of odd disguises. *United Ireland* editor William O'Brien once encountered Parnell skulking in a foggy London park, wearing a "bizarre" duck-hunting outfit.

Determined to stay married to Katharine so as to be able to share in the substantial inheritance that she would receive when Mrs. Wood died, O'Shea recognized that withdrawing from politics would leave him at less risk of having the true nature of his domestic situation exposed. He especially feared being exposed to the world as a voluntary cuckold. Katharine, for her part, could not afford to have the relationship made public because she knew that Mrs. Wood would not include her in her will if she found out about it. The pretense that Parnell was just a friend of the O'Sheas would have to be maintained until Mrs. Wood died, and since Mrs. Wood had now reached the age of 93, Parnell and the O'Sheas naturally imagined that the pretense would not have to be maintained for very much longer.

From the spring of 1886 onward, Parnell and Katharine went to increasingly great lengths to keep their relationship a secret. They moved from one rented house to another, and Parnell himself assumed a succession of aliases in his dealings with landlords, tradesmen, and neighbors. For a man in his position, he was taking an extraordinary risk in continuing the relationship, and he knew it.

7

Statesman Under Suspicion

On March 26, 1886, Gladstone, who that year was elected to serve his third term as prime minister, presented the draft of his proposed home rule legislation — the Government of Ireland Bill — to the cabinet. The two cabinet ministers who were diehard opponents of home rule, Chamberlain and Secretary for Scotland Sir George Trevelyan, immediately resigned in protest. This development did not make Gladstone's task any easier, but the prime minister refused to be intimidated.

On April 5, three days before the Government of Ireland Bill was introduced in the House of Commons, Gladstone invited Parnell to meet him for preliminary discussions about it. This was the first time the two men had met in private. Their conversation dealt mainly with the financial aspects of the bill, which were extremely complicated, and Gladstone, himself an exceptionally brilliant man, was quite disconcerted by the rapidity with which Parnell absorbed their intricacies.

> *It is not now a question of self-government for Ireland, it is only a question as to how much of the self-goverment they will be able to cheat us out of.*
> —PARNELL
> following the fall of the Conservative government in January 1886

On April 18, 1887, the *Times* of London published a facsimile of a letter, allegedly written by Parnell, that condoned and implicated him in the Phoenix Park murders. Parnell was called before a special commission to stand trial and the Home Rule cause was in jeopardy again.

Home Rule M.P. and *United Ireland* editor William O'-Brien was one of the men who were responsible for organizing and maintaining the new land agitation, called the Plan of Campaign, which was set in motion during the winter of 1886—87.

The Government of Ireland Bill proposed that Ireland have a parliament of its own, that the Irish executive be accountable to the new parliament in matters of domestic policy, and that no Irish M.P.s be retained at Westminster following the institution of the new parliament. Furthermore, the Irish parliament would not be permitted to subsidize any religion or to control the customs and excise service. It would have two "orders" — a partly elected upper house, in which representatives of the propertied classes would predominate, and a more democratic, fully representative lower house. The Parliament at Westminster would remain in control of Irish foreign policy, and Ireland would continue to be defended, and garrisoned, by the British armed forces. The RIC would remain under imperial control for several years following the establishment of the Irish parliament. Ireland would also pay a fifteenth of the imperial revenue (the tax, paid by Britain's colonies, that financed the imperial administration).

Having scrutinized the bill, Parnell informed Gladstone that he strongly opposed four of its provisions. He wanted the proposed Dublin parliament to control both the RIC and the customs and excise service. Ireland's imperial contribution, he suggested, should be set at a twentieth or a twenty-first part of the total. Parnell also asserted that the Dublin parliament should have a single chamber, not two. Gladstone noted Parnell's comments but gave no assurances that he would alter the bill.

On the afternoon of April 8, Parnell outlined his reservations about the Government of Ireland Bill in a speech to the House of Commons. He qualified his opposition to the bill as it then stood with a statement to the effect that the Irish people and their representatives would accept the bill as an adequate settlement of the home rule question if it were amended to their satisfaction.

Irish nationalists in Ireland, England, and the United States greeted the bill with great enthusiasm, but their euphoria was not to last. By the end of May, when debate on the second reading of the bill had been in progress for two weeks, it had become apparent that Gladstone stood little chance of getting the bill passed. Within the Liberal party, the Radicals and the Whigs had mustered enough allies in their campaign against the bill to ensure that the government would be unable to command a majority in favor of the bill in the House of Commons. On May 28, Gladstone announced that he intended to withdraw the bill and reintroduce it — with amendments devised in response to the comments of its British critics — in the fall. But on May 31, Chamberlain and 50 other Liberal critics of the bill decided to vote against the second reading anyway. When the House of Commons voted on the second reading on June 8, the bill was rejected by 343 votes to 313. The 93 Liberals who voted against the government then reconstituted themselves as a new party, the Liberal Unionists, under Chamberlain's leadership.

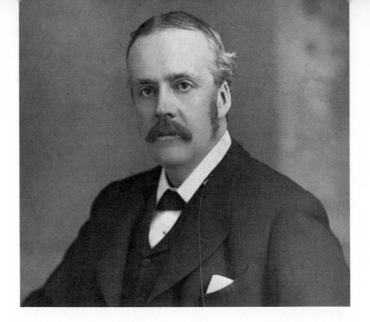

Arthur ("Bloody") Balfour, chief secretary for Ireland during the Plan of Campaign, was determined to crush the land-reform movement as quickly as possible. "I shall be as relentless as Cromwell," he declared, "in enforcing the obedience to the law."

Parnell's contribution to the heated debate that preceded the vote was masterful. He recognized, however, that nothing he said would affect the final outcome. "I now repeat," he declared, "what I have already said on the first reading . . . that we look upon the provisions of the bill as a final settlement of this question, and that I believe that the Irish people have accepted it as such a settlement." With this declaration, Parnell essentially disowned his earlier assertions that he could not guarantee that, under home rule, the Irish would not seek to go beyond legislative independence to full independence as a sovereign republic.

The subsequent general election necessitated by the Liberal government's defeat was fought mainly on the issue of home rule. Parnell was now prepared to make an alliance with the Liberals the centerpiece of his entire political strategy. In so doing, he abandoned the principle of independent opposition, under which the Home Rule party had drawn closer to whichever of the two British parties seemed more likely to concede home rule. Parnell realized that the principle of independent opposition was valid only when *both* British parties were prepared to discuss home rule. Now that the Conservatives had utterly rejected home rule, the principle of independent opposition no longer made sense. The Home Rule party had no choice but to ally with the Liberals — the only British party that supported home rule.

The general election gave the Unionist (anti–Home Rule) forces a stunning victory: The Conservatives and the anti–Home Rule Liberals won a total of 394 seats. The Home Rule party won 85 seats. The Liberals took only 191. The government that Salisbury then formed thus enjoyed a majority of 118.

In August 1886 the Home Rule party attempted to persuade the government to institute a relief program for Ireland's farmers, who were once again in dire economic straits due to increased competition from American agriculture. The delegates to a Home Rule party meeting in Dublin passed a resolution informing the government that Ireland's farmers were no longer in a position to pay the rents fixed by the land court back in 1881–82. Parnell then introduced a Tenants' Relief Bill in the House of Commons, but it was rejected by a majority of 95 votes. The Irish leader now had to face the fact that a new land war, which he had been trying hard to avoid, had become inevitable. As the situation in Ireland deteriorated once again, Parnell worked to convince British supporters of Irish nationalism that the blame for the impending violence rested squarely with the government, not with the people of Ireland. So as not to alienate the Liberals, Parnell also continued to advocate moderation, even though his more radical colleagues, some of whom were already preparing for a new land agitation, were by now convinced that the time for moderation was past.

The new land agitation, known as the Plan of Campaign, was initiated in October 1886. Under the terms of the plan — which was originally conceived by Dillon and systematized by Home Rule M.P. and INL secretary Timothy Harrington — dissatisfied tenants on selected estates were to join together and offer the landlords what they considered a fair rent. If the landlord rejected the offer, the tenants were to pay him nothing. Instead, they would put their "fair rents" into an estate fund. The independent trustees of the estate fund would then dole out allowances from the fund to those tenants who suffered eviction.

A Plan of Campaign march proceeds by torchlight from Kingstown to Dublin. While the Plan of Campaign gathered momentum, Parnell attempted to distance himself from it, fearing that his political credibility in Parliament would be compromised by the violence.

As the Plan of Campaign gathered momentum during the winter of 1886–87, Parnell found it increasingly difficult to strike a balance in his attitude toward the new land agitation that would neither alienate its backers in the Home Rule party nor damage the party's relations with the Liberals. It was only when Home Rule M.P.s involved in the Plan of Campaign started making inflammatory statements that offended public opinion in Britain that Parnell made it clear that he did not support the Plan of Campaign. In December 1886, he summoned William O'Brien from Dublin and informed him of his conviction that the Plan of Campaign should remain confined to a limited number of estates and not become any more violent. His own policies, Parnell said, would suffer if the agitation resulted in the renewal of coercion. Parnell feared that the Liberals, who were already complaining about the Plan of Campaign, might break off the alliance if the agitation were to be extended to estates other than those on which it was presently in operation.

As he worked to preserve the Liberal–Home Rule alliance and to prevent the Plan of Campaign from

becoming as great an agitation as the one the INLL had conducted seven years earlier, Parnell became increasingly prone to anxiety and depression, both of which were aggravated by the strain of the constant subterfuge to which he was forced to resort in his efforts to keep his relationship with Katharine O'Shea secret. It was also during the winter of 1886–87 that Parnell first became seriously ill with the kidney disorder known as Bright's disease, which frequently left him feeling weak and caused him to lose a considerable amount of weight.

In the spring of 1887, the government finally moved against the Plan of Campaign, which was attracting massive popular support throughout Ireland. On March 28, Arthur Balfour, the new chief secretary for Ireland, introduced the repressive Criminal Law Amendment Bill, which made virtually every activity central to the Plan of Campaign — boycotting, intimidation, withholding of rent, and resistance to eviction, to name but a few — illegal. As the bill proceeded through Parliament, the Home Rulers maintained a staunch campaign of obstruction, but to no avail — the Criminal Law Amendment Bill became law in July.

Parnell's hard-fought battle against Balfour's coercive legislation was made considerably more difficult because his own credibility as an advocate of constitutionalism had come under attack early on in the struggle. On April 18, 1887, the *Times* of London, which had started running a series of articles under the general heading of "Parnellism and Crime" in March of that same year, published a facsimile of a letter — dated May 15, 1882 — apparently signed by Parnell and expressing approval of the murder of Undersecretary Burke in Phoenix Park.

The incriminating letter was one of several that had been given to the *Times* by Edward Caulfield Houston, the secretary of the Irish Loyal and Patriotic Union, Ireland's premier Unionist organization. The letters themselves were the work of an Irish journalist named Richard Pigott — the same Pigott from whom Parnell had purchased the newspapers that had merged as *United Ireland*. Houston, who wanted to discredit the Parnellites, had originally commissioned Pigott to write a pamphlet proving that there was a connection between Parnellism and crime. Pigott, having failed to find any evidence that such a link existed, had resorted to forgery so as to continue receiving money from Houston, who believed that the letters were genuine and hoped that their publication would make the passage of the Criminal Law Amendment Bill much easier.

In July 1888 the political game in which Parnell and his colleagues were involved became particularly dirty. Early that month, the libel suit that Home Rule M.P. Frank Hugh O'Donnell had brought against the *Times* in 1887 for portraying him as an advocate of violence in the "Parnellism and Crime" articles finally came to court. O'Donnell's attorney took the unorthodox step of not requesting his client to deliver testimony in his own defense, thereby losing the case. As a result, the attorney for the *Times*, Sir Richard Webster, was able to repeat all the newspaper's original accusations, as well as several new ones, without being contradicted. Webster also produced further incriminating letters supposedly written by Parnell and other INLL leaders.

Having inspected the incriminating documents at Webster's offices, Parnell denounced them as forgeries. Determined to clear his name, he demanded a House of Commons select committee be established to prove or disprove the *Times*'s allegations. Leading Conservative W. H. Smith, who held the position of leader of the House of Commons, suggested that the government might be prepared to establish a commission of inquiry, comprising mainly judges, to investigate "the allegations and charges made against certain Members of Parliament" by the defendants in O'Donnell's lawsuit.

Parnell did not object to Smith's suggestion, even though the proposed commission would be charged with investigating more material than the letters that had been the subject of his original complaint. On July 16 the Irish leader justifiably became suspicious, however, when Smith, acting on behalf of the government, moved to introduce the legislation that would establish the commission—the Members of Parliament (Charges and Allegations) Bill, which

In February 1889, under cross-examination by Parnell's attorney, Sir Charles Russell (standing, left), pornographer Richard Pigott (standing, right) is exposed as the forger of the letters implicating Parnell in the Phoenix Park murders.

Parnell emerged from the forged letter scandal and the Plan of Campaign years unscathed and at the height of his popularity in Ireland. He was called the Uncrowned King of Ireland, and it seemed to the Irish people that it was only a matter of time before Parnell secured a home rule agreement from Gladstone.

is generally referred to as the Special Commission Bill — before it had even been printed and circulated in the House of Commons. Smith merely informed the House of Commons that the bill accorded with the proposal he had made to Parnell on July 12. The situation became even more dubious on July 17, when the government widened the terms of the inquiry by proposing to investigate "the allegations and charges made against certain Members of Parliament and *other persons*. . . ." That the Conservative government viewed the proceedings it wished to set in motion as a trial of the entire nationalist movement — the "other persons" — rather than an investigation of specific allegations was now apparent to everyone.

In September 1888 the Special Commission set to work. Two groups of people were under investigation: 65 Home Rule M.P.s and 67 "other persons" — Irish and Irish-American — with whom the M.P.s were alleged to have associated. The charges against them were that they had conspired to achieve absolute independence for Ireland; that they had attempted, in conducting an agrarian agitation, to destroy the landlord system; and that in furtherance of those aims they had committed crimes or had been accomplices in crime. The most important question, however, continued to be the one that had sparked the investigation: Was Parnell the author of the incriminating letters or not?

The question finally received an answer on February 21, 1889, when Pigott, who had been named as the source of the letters by Houston following the introduction of the Special Commission Bill, was cross-examined by Sir Charles Russell, Parnell's attorney. Russell already had information suggesting that the letters were forgeries and that Pigott was the forger. Having noticed that in one of the letters published by the *Times* the word *hesitancy* had been misspelled, Russell asked Pigott to write some words on a sheet of paper. The last of the five words that Russell asked Pigott to write down was *hesitancy*. The hapless Pigott duly complied and provided Russell with evidence that convinced him he was on the right track. Pigott wrote not *hesitancy* but *hesitency* — the very same misspelling of the word that had appeared in the facsimile letter. From that point on, Russell hounded Pigott mercilessly. By the afternoon of the following day — Friday, February 22 — Russell had completely destroyed Pigott's credibility and reputation. On Monday, February 25, the disgraced forger fled the country, heading for Madrid, Spain. Later that week, in a hotel room in Madrid, Pigott put the barrel of a revolver in his mouth and pulled the trigger. Parnell's name had been cleared.

The *Times*'s attempt to discredit Parnell and the entire Irish nationalist movement had backfired. The public now perceived the Irish leader as a victim, an honorable and courageous man battling overwhelming odds, and virtually overnight he became more popular in Britain than he had ever been before. Parnell had now reached the zenith of his career. On March 1, 1889, he appeared in the House of Commons for the first time since his exoneration. The Liberals and the Home Rulers rose to their feet as one and gave him a standing ovation.

Parnell's increased power and prestige were not to last for very long, however. During the next two years, the Irish leader would be pursuing his policies in what would prove to have been a calm before a storm. The Special Commission's official report, which was published in February 1890, exonerated the INLL leaders from the charges of criminal association. The judges did, however, find some of the respondents — including Davitt, Dillon, and O'Brien — guilty of having established or joined the INLL intending to use it to secure Irish independence. Parnell's comment on the verdict justifiably implied that the judges had reached a conclusion that had been obvious to everyone long before they started their deliberations. "Really," he declared, "between ourselves, I think it is just about what I would have said myself."

The Special Commission's findings were almost a year away when Parnell was vindicated. This meant, as Parnell biographer F. S. L. Lyons notes, that between February 1889 and February 1890, "the Irish leaders, and Parnell especially, remained under a shadow which held their whole political movement in suspense."

May I venture to suggest as an alternative that I should not be asked to come forward but be provided with means to leave the country?
—RICHARD PIGOTT
forger, in a November 1888 letter to leading Unionist Edward Caulfield Houston

8

"God Help Ireland"

On December 18, 1889, Parnell met with Gladstone at Hawarden, the Liberal leader's country home. The two men discussed Gladstone's latest ideas on the subject of home rule, and when they ended their talk later that same day, both were satisfied that the alliance between their respective parties would continue to be close and constructive. The Home Rulers and the Liberals alike considered Parnell's visit to Hawarden convincing evidence of the great esteem in which the former prime minister held the Irish leader. Unfortunately for Parnell, however, just six days after his visit to Hawarden, the event that signaled the beginning of the end of his career occurred: On December 24, 1889, Captain O'Shea petitioned for divorce, citing Parnell as corespondent.

O'Shea had made his move as part of his strategy of seeking, in collaboration with Katharine's brothers and sisters, to overturn Mrs. Wood's will. The seemingly indestructible old lady had died, of natural causes, in May 1889, leaving her entire fortune to Katharine under a legal arrangement that denied

Mrs. O'Shea will be your ruin.
—content of a telegram sent from Joseph Biggar to Parnell on February 7, 1889

Parnell was riding high on a wave of popularity and political momentum as 1889 drew to a close, so his fall from grace seemed all the more sudden, violent, and total. On December 24, 1889, Captain O'Shea filed for divorce and named Parnell in the suit; by October 6, 1891, the Chief had given his final speech in Ireland.

Captain O'Shea any entitlement to a share of the money. Because the will was being contested, it had become the subject of a case in probate court. Under British law, this meant that the court would hold Mrs. Wood's money in escrow until the case was settled. Having been cut out of the will, Captain O'Shea now recognized that only by destroying Katharine's reputation in divorce court and thus weakening her case in probate court would he stand a chance of securing a share of her inheritance.

News of O'Shea's petition spread quickly. Parnell himself made no attempt to deny that O'Shea had a case. The Irish leader wanted the divorce to go through as quickly as possible so that he could finally marry Katharine.

The divorce case came to court on December 15, 1890. Because neither Parnell nor Katharine contested the case, Captain O'Shea's attorney was able, without fear of contradiction, to portray the Irish leader and his mistress in the worst possible light, accusing them of having systematically deceived his client. On December 17 the court awarded Captain O'Shea a decree *nisi* (taking effect at a specified time unless modified by further proceedings). The court also awarded Captain O'Shea custody of all of Mrs. O'Shea's children who were under age 16. O'Shea thus became the legal guardian of Katie and Clare O'Shea, Parnell's daughters by Katharine. Parnell, having been found guilty of adultery, now stood condemned as an offender against the strict moral standards of the period. But the anguish that the loss of his children caused Parnell, combined with his pride and his conviction that he was indispensable to Irish nationalism, do much to explain the grim determination that he displayed in the fight that followed.

A storm of hostility toward Parnell erupted within the Liberal party, and several Home Rule M.P.s secretly began to fear that Parnell's predicament might possibly destroy their own party. The most progressive section of the Liberal party, the Gladstonian, or mainstream, Liberals, did not believe that private matters should influence public affairs. However, the Gladstonians found themselves facing a barrage of criticism from Liberal voters of the Nonconformist persuasion, who found the Gladstonians' refusal to condemn Parnell on moral grounds offensive. The highly moralistic, socially conservative, and predominantly working-class Nonconformists — members of England's "free," or non-Anglican Protestant churches — were much less forgiving than the Gladstonians where matters of personal morality were concerned. Savage attacks on Parnell began appearing in those Liberal newspapers with largely Nonconformist readerships, and Gladstone quickly realized that a large proportion of his own party would almost certainly reject the Liberal-nationalist alliance if Parnell were to remain head of the Home Rule party.

That the Nonconformists would force Gladstone's hand had been apparent to Davitt — a dedicated socialist who understood the English working class better than any other Irish nationalist — from the moment the divorce hearings ended. On November 20, Davitt's newspaper, the *Labour World*, published a demand that for the good of the party Parnell withdraw from public life for a few months.

Coal miners labor in a mine in Staffordshire, England. Many of the members of the predominantly working-class faction of the Liberal party were coal miners. The Nonconformists launched some of the most virulent attacks on Parnell during the Kitty O'Shea scandal.

Home Rule M.P.s voted 45 to 28 for the resignation of Chairman Parnell on December 6, 1890, in Committee Room 15 of the House of Commons. Parnell blamed much of his downfall on Gladstone. "You know as well as I do that Gladstone always loathed me," he said to Katharine O'Shea.

Davitt particularly wanted to ensure that Parnell should not secure an eve-of-session reelection as party chairman for the forthcoming parliamentary session. In a letter to William J. Walsh, the archbishop of Dublin, written on November 20, Davitt declared: "Now *why* cannot Parnell retire for this session? Is he going to force himself and his paramour upon Ireland at the expense of Home Rule? . . . If he appears . . . at the opening of parliament as the *newly elected* leader of the Irish people, goodbye for this generation to Home Rule, and God help Ireland."

Davitt's bitter and brooding words were prophetic. On November 22, Gladstone received a letter from Harcourt informing him of the mood of the delegates at a recent meeting of the National Liberal Federation. Harcourt noted that Parnell had been condemned not just by the more moralistic delegates but by everybody else at the conference. The delegates, he said, had come to the conclusion that the Liberals should abandon their alliance with the nationalists if Parnell remained head of the Home Rule party. On November 24, Gladstone wrote a letter to leading Liberal politician John Morley and asked him to show it to Parnell the following day, before the Home Rule party's eve-of-session meeting. In the letter, Gladstone argued that Parnell's reelection to the chairmanship of the Home Rule party would "not only place many hearty and effective friends of the Irish cause in a position of great embarrassment, but would render my retention of the leadership of the liberal party, based as it has mainly been upon the prosecution of the Irish cause, almost a nullity." Also on November 24, Gladstone sent for McCarthy and informed him of the position he intended to take with regard to Parnell. The Liberal leader stressed that Parnell's retention of the leadership would guarantee a Liberal defeat at the next general election, thus consigning further efforts to implement home rule to the dim and distant future. In other words, Gladstone had decided that Parnell would have to go.

Neither Morley nor McCarthy managed to contact Parnell prior to the eve-of-session meeting. Once the meeting began, McCarthy found it impossible to summon up the courage to inform Parnell of Gladstone's ultimatum. As a result, the Home Rulers remained unaware of Gladstone's position and reelected Parnell by acclamation. When Morley discovered what had happened, he showed Gladstone's letter to Parnell; the Irish leader responded by announcing that he had no intention of resigning.

On December 15, 1890, Parnell arrived in Dublin. A huge crowd of supporters gathered beneath the statue of Irish nationalist hero Daniel O'Connell. When Parnell appeared, according to Irish poet Katharine Tynan, "The great gathering rose at him . . . there was a sea of passionate faces, loving, admiring, almost worshipping that pale man."

Parnell addresses his constituents from a balcony of the Victoria Hotel at Cork. The two factions of the Home Rule party, the Parnellites and the anti-Parnellites, fought bitterly for the support of the people of Cork.

Morley immediately stormed off to give the bad news to Gladstone, who quickly decided that the time had come to put the issue before the public. The Liberal leader arranged for his letter to Morley to be published the following day in the *Pall Mall Gazette*, an influential London newspaper.

With the letter's publication, the great political machine that Parnell had created fell to pieces. Party members who still supported Parnell resented what they saw as an attempt by Gladstone and the Liberals to dictate to the party, whereas those who did not contended that Parnell should resign for the sake of the Liberal-nationalist alliance, which had to be preserved at all costs.

On November 28, at a meeting attended mainly by his own supporters, he read aloud a manifesto entitled "To the People of Ireland." In the first section of this controversial document, Parnell accused Gladstone of trying to dictate the Home Rule party's choice of leader and gave an account of the Hawarden negotiations that distorted everything that Gladstone had said on the occasion, as the Liberal leader quickly pointed out when he learned of the manifesto's contents. In the second section, Parnell portrayed the proposals for a future Home Rule Bill that Gladstone had made at Hawarden as indicating that the Liberals were unreliable, and he stressed that the Home Rule party should maintain its independence. If the Home Rule party's pursuit of an independent policy led to a Liberal defeat at the next election, Parnell asserted in concluding, the resulting postponement of Home Rule would, in his opinion, "be preferable to a compromise of our national rights by the acceptance of a measure which would not realize the aspirations of our race."

When the manifesto became public knowledge, people immediately began to ask why Parnell had continued to support the Liberal-nationalist alliance following the Hawarden negotiations if, as he now claimed, he had had reservations about the proposals Gladstone had made on that occasion. The Irish leader's response to this question was that "it was impossible for me to disclose by public speech or by private explanation the setback which the Hawarden communications had given to the cause of Home Rule. . . . The matter was still not definitely settled. Until all hope had been removed of arriving at a satisfactory undertaking upon these important subjects with Mr. Gladstone it would have been highly improper for me . . . to have referred publicly to the matter, and it would have been difficult for me to have selected from amongst my colleagues for the purpose of a disclosure." Few people found this argument convincing, and Parnell's credibility deteriorated still further when Gladstone published his own, highly detailed account of the negotiations, which revealed the distorted and self-serving nature of Parnell's account.

On November 30 the five Home Rule M.P.s who had earlier telegraphed a message of support for Parnell from the United States sent a telegram urging the party to reject him. Demands for a change of party leader were also forthcoming from Archbishop Croke and Archbishop Walsh. Like many other nationalists in the Irish Catholic hierarchy, they felt impelled to come out against Parnell now that Gladstone had effectively declared that the Irish would have to choose between Parnell and home rule —that they could not have both.

A special party meeting requested by the anti-Parnellite faction convened on December 1 in Committee Room 15 in the House of Commons. The bitter debate between the two groups raged on and on and finally disintegrated on the sixth day, when the meeting was on the verge of turning into a brawl. Timothy Healy, responding to Parnellite John Redmond's cry that Parnell was the "master of the party," made a tasteless and provocative reference to Katharine O'Shea: "Who," Healy yelled, "is to be the mistress of the party?" Recognizing that the situation was now irretrievable, McCarthy stepped forward and announced that he considered further participation in a discussion that had come to contain only "reproach, ill-temper, controversy and indignity" absolutely useless and that all who felt as he did should leave the room. McCarthy's statement was a call for secession by the anti-Parnellites, and a few minutes later he and 44 others walked out, leaving Parnell with 28 followers. The party that Parnell had forged into the most effective political machine in the history of the United Kingdom had rejected him. Within hours of the split, the Parnellites and the anti-Parnellites began making preparations for the most important battle of all — the fight for the hearts and minds of the Irish.

On December 9, 1890, Parnell and several members of his faction set out from London for Ireland. Shortly before his departure, he was asked by a reporter from the *Freeman's Journal* if he had a message for the Irish people. "Tell them," Parnell replied, "that I will fight to the end."

Parnell kept his promise. On December 10 he arrived in Dublin, where he was greeted by a vast crowd of his supporters, some of whom immediately demonstrated their devotion to him by beating up the hapless Healy, who had made the mistake of traveling aboard the same train as Parnell. The crowd then followed Parnell to the building that housed the offices of *United Ireland*, which was then being run by its deputy editor, Matthew Bodkin, who had recently published an editorial criticizing Parnell. The Irish leader, determined to reassert his control over the newspaper, strode into Bodkin's office and summarily dismissed him. The deputy editor stood his ground, informing Parnell that he had no right to dismiss him. The standoff was finally resolved by a Fenian member of Parnell's entourage, who gave Bodkin the choice of walking out of the office or being carried out. Bodkin decided to leave voluntarily.

Later that same day, Parnell gave one of the most brilliant oratorical performances of his life at the Rotunda, Dublin's premier meeting hall, hammering his audience with a pithy and forceful exposition of his contention that the principle of independent opposition should now resume its former position as a core element of the Home Rule party's approach to parliamentary politics. The applause that had punctuated his address from the outset grew even more thunderous when Parnell suggested that parliamentary politics alone might not suffice to secure legislative independence. This sudden reversion to the radicalism that had propelled him from obscurity to prominence at the beginning of his career galvanized the entire audience. "I have not misled you," he declared. "I have never said that this constitutional movement must succeed. . . . And if Ireland leaves this path upon which I have led her . . . I will not for my part say that I will not accompany her further."

The following morning, Parnell learned that a group of anti-Parnellites had reoccupied the offices of *United Ireland* during the night. The Irish leader immediately rounded up a gang of his supporters and took a carriage to the newspaper's offices, traveling at breakneck speed. Upon arriving, Parnell stormed up the steps and began pounding on the door. Having failed to elicit a response, he began demolishing the door with a crowbar supplied by one of his supporters.

When the door finally fell from its hinges, Parnell and his companions charged inside and raced up the stairs to the editorial offices. There they mauled the handful of anti-Parnellites who had volunteered to attempt a holding action while their colleagues beat a hasty retreat via the back door. Parnell then strode to a window overlooking the street and addressed the crowd that had gathered outside. A bystander interviewed by Parnell biographer Barry

> *[Parnell] brought Ireland within sight of the Promised Land. The triumph of the national cause awaits other times, and another man.*
> —RICHARD BARRY O'BRIEN
> Irish nationalist
> and author

Parnell gave a speech in a driving rainstorm at Kilkenny in September 1891. Physically and emotionally exhausted from the traumas of the previous year, Parnell became ill after giving the speech; he collapsed in his home soon after.

O'Brien gave the following account of what happened next: "The enthusiasm which greeted him cannot be described. His face was ghastly pale. . . . His hat was off now, his hair dishevelled, the dust of the conflict begrimed his well-brushed coat. . . . For myself, I felt a thrill of dread, as if I looked at a tiger in the frenzy of its rage. Then he spoke, and the tone of his voice was even more terrible than his look. He was brief, rapid, decisive, and the closing words of his speech still ring in my ear: 'I rely on Dublin. Dublin is true. What Dublin says to-day Ireland will say to-morrow.' "

Having thus recaptured *United Ireland*, Parnell caught a train to Cork, where he intended to set up a base of operations for a by-election contest in the nearby town of Kilkenny. The anti-Parnellite candidate in the by-election was a former colonial governor named Sir John Pope-Hennessy.

Once established in Cork, Parnell staged a succession of rallies. In the speeches he gave, he began to sound a new theme, informing his audiences that he intended to make the working class the basis of his national support. In so doing, Parnell in effect turned his back on the businessmen and lawyers who had long been the mainstay of the home rule movement and who predominated in the party faction that had rejected him.

Parnell fought a savage campaign in Kilkenny, as, too, did Healy and the other anti-Parnellites. Parnell's relentless emphasis on the importance of a renewed policy of independent opposition, combined with his provocative intimations that a much tougher line could be taken if constitutionalism failed, began to attract considerable numbers of Fenians to his cause. This trend had become apparent at the beginning of December, when James Stephens, John O'Leary, and John Devoy — three of the most influential Fenians of their day — declared their support for Parnell. To many people it now seemed the Irish leader had reverted to radicalism, forsaking the gains that he had secured for Irish nationalism in the constitutional arena during the previous 10 years.

Parnell also had to face the opposition of the Irish Catholic clergy, many of whom were now working furiously on behalf of the anti-Parnellites. Ultimately, the Catholic clergy's opposition to Parnell proved as decisive in his downfall as it had in aiding his rise to supremacy. Throughout 1890, the Irish Catholic hierarchy had accused the Parnellites of ignoring the importance of clerical support and of forsaking their earlier promise to uphold Catholic interests in their eagerness to ingratiate themselves with the Liberals. On July 31 of that year, Michael Logue, the archbishop of Armagh, had written a letter to Archbishop Walsh. In his communication, Archbishop Logue asserted that the Parnellites had "climbed to their present influential positions on the shoulders of Irish priests and Irish bishops. It was the priests who worked up the [electoral] registers for them, the priests who fought the elections. . . . They [the Parnellites] . . . think they are secure enough to kick away the ladder by which they mounted." Now, in December 1890, the priests took their revenge, using their influence to turn the people against Parnell. When the results of the Kilkenny by-election were announced, it became apparent that Parnell had suffered a stunning defeat, winning only 1,362 votes to Pope-Hennessy's 2,527.

Throughout the early months of 1891, Parnell maintained a rigorous schedule. During the week he attended to parliamentary business in London; on weekends he traveled to Ireland and delivered speeches in towns and villages throughout the country. His health, which had been deteriorating steadily throughout the party split and the Kilkenny by-election, grew worse. Gradually, his speeches became stale. Parnell even stooped to preaching the gospel of republicanism to goad the crowds to greater frenzy.

The only innovations that Parnell made while fighting to regain his former supremacy were an attempt to attract English and Irish working-class voters to his cause and an attempt to address the perennial problem of the position of Protestants in Irish politics. The Irish leader made his first overture to England's workers in March 1891, in London. Parnell called for shorter hours in the coal-mining industry, state control of selected public services, and improved relations between labor and management. A few days later, speaking at a gathering of trade unionists in Dublin, Parnell expressed approval of the progressive demands put forward at the meeting. These included manhood suffrage (one man, one vote), land nationalization, an eight-hour workday, state control of transport, and improved conditions in the factories. The Liberals and the conservatives speedily condemned Parnell's overtures to the working class as opportunism. The Irish leader's new policy also came under fire from Davitt, who resented Parnell's encroachment on an area of politics that he himself had considered his exclusive domain of expertise.

The demise of nationalist unity enabled Parnell to express his true feelings on Ulster Unionism and Irish Protestantism, feelings that he had been obliged to keep to himself during his tenure as party leader for fear of alienating his predominantly Catholic constituents. Breaking with the Catholic nationalism that he had once championed, Parnell now revealed that he preferred a broader nonsectarian and thoroughly secular nationalism — the kind of secular nationalism that was one of the three fundamentals of Fenianism. (Parnell did not, as has been noted, approve of the other two fundamentals of Fenianism—republicanism and physical force.)

Parnell also revealed his conviction that the depth of the sectarian divisions in Irish society would render the emergence of an Irish nationalism with no sectarian characteristics virtually impossible. Prior to the split, his concern with the place of Protestants, and especially the Ulster Unionists, in Irish national life had been directed mainly toward the Protestants of southern Ireland, the sector of society from which he himself came. After the split, which fractured Catholic nationalism, Parnell began to pay more attention to the other, much older and more problematic divide in Irish society — the divide that separated the Catholic nationalists from the Ulster Unionists, who had always equated home rule with, as they themselves put it, "Rome rule."

In Belfast in May 1891, Parnell gave perhaps the most important speech of his political career. In it he declared,

> . . . it is the duty of the [Catholic] majority [in Ireland as a whole] to leave no stone unturned . . . to conciliate . . . the [Protestant] minority. I think the majority have always been inclined to go a long way in this direction; but it has been undoubtedly true that every Irish patriot has always recognized . . . from the time of [18th-century Irish republican revolutionary Theobald] Wolfe Tone until now that until the religious prejudices of the minority, whether reasonable or unreasonable, are conciliated . . . Ireland can never enjoy perfect freedom, Ireland can never be united; and until Ireland is practically united, so long as there is a large [Protestant] majority [in northeastern Ulster] . . . in Belfast a considerable [Protestant] majority . . . so long as there is this important [Protestant] minority [in Ireland as a whole] who consider, rightly or wrongly — I believe and feel sure wrongly — that the concession of legitimate freedom to Ireland means harm and damage to them . . . the work of building up an independent Ireland will have upon it a fatal clog and a fatal drag. I do not know . . . whether there are any elements in the present struggle [within the Home Rule movement] which are likely to estrange the [Protestant] minority more than they have been. I trust that there are not. I trust that all Irishmen who take part in this struggle on one side or the other will . . . try to avoid doing anything to attach to this fight more than is possible, or more than is legitimate, of a sectarian or a religious aspect."

Charles and Katharine Parnell's house on the sea in Brighton, England. Parnell and Katharine lived here together as man and wife for only five months before Parnell died.

Coming from a politician in whose destruction the Roman Catholic church had played a major role, the last sentence of Parnell's speech was magnanimous, to say the least. And it should be noted that the conciliation Parnell demanded has never been achieved and that Ireland remains divided to this day. A statesman capable of rectifying this unfortunate situation has yet to emerge, and should such a statesman ever appear, he will have to deal with the same hard truths that Parnell so forcefully expounded in Belfast nearly a century ago.

The ranks of Parnell's supporters continued to dwindle. An increasing number of Irishmen were coming to the conclusion that the Liberal-nationalist alliance was more valuable to Ireland than was Parnell. As Lyons notes, "It was one thing to overlook Parnell's relations with Mrs. O'Shea, but quite another thing to overlook his relations with Gladstone after the latter had made it clear that his [Parnell's] continuance at the head of the Irish party jeopardized, not merely the Liberal-nationalist alliance, but Home Rule itself. It was this threat, rather than the bishops' condemnation, which stripped Parnell of his support in the country."

Parnell married Katharine O'Shea on June 25, 1891, at a register office in Steyning, a small town a few miles from Brighton, the resort on England's southern coast where he and Katharine were living. Given the circumstances, it was not a happy occasion, and the Irish bishops did their best to make it even more difficult by condemning Parnell for marrying a divorcée. They issued a resolution recording "the solemn expression of our judgement, as pastors of the Irish people, that Mr. Parnell, by his public misconduct, has utterly disqualified himself to be their leader. . . . We . . . feel bound on this occasion to call on our people to repudiate his leadership."

In July 1891, Parnell met with the worst defeat he had yet suffered in a by-election, in Carlow, Ireland. The anti-Parnellite candidate won by 3,755 votes to 1,539. That same month brought further evidence that Parnell's base of support was crumbling. A mere 1,600 people attended an INL convention that the Irish leader had called in Dublin. At the same time, the circulation of the *Freeman's Journal*, which had continued to support Parnell, was falling dramatically. Disappointed but undeterred, Parnell continued to travel the length and breadth of the country on the weekends, delivering a succession of increasingly bitter speeches. It was now apparent that the battle was lost, however, and Parnell's physical and mental health were deteriorating so fast that many became convinced that he might soon be forced to retire from politics whether he wanted to or not.

Historian Robert Kee best summed up what Parnell's tragic death meant for Ireland. He wrote, "The chance of Home Rule for the next twenty years was buried with him."

Parnell gave the last speech he ever made in Ireland, at Creggs, a small village in county Roscommon, in September 1891. His Dublin physician, concerned at the turn for the worse that Parnell's health had taken a week earlier when the Irish leader gave a speech at an open-air meeting during a rainstorm, had advised him to stay home, but Parnell had refused. After speaking at Creggs, Parnell returned to Dublin, where he spent a few days dealing with the impending launch of his new newspaper, the *Irish Daily Independent*. On September 30, ignoring his physician's warning that he was not fit enough to travel, Parnell boarded a ferry to England. On the afternoon of October 1, he arrived in Brighton. Later that same day, his condition grew worse: Suddenly, Parnell found that his legs would barely support him, and he had to ask Katharine to help him mount the stairs to his bedroom. On October 3, Parnell became so ill that Katharine summoned a doctor, who managed to ease Parnell's rheumatic pains but could do little else. Parnell spent the next three days alternating between delirium and clarity whenever he was awake. When he slept, he slept badly, tossing and turning incessantly. On October 6, just before 12:00 P.M., Charles Stewart Parnell, the greatest Irish nationalist politician of his generation, died of heart failure at age 46, breathing his last in the arms of the woman he loved.

Parnell's funeral took place in Dublin on the afternoon of October 11, 1891. Thousands of mourners from all over Ireland followed his coffin from Dublin's city hall, where it had lain in state earlier in the day, to the Glasnevin cemetery.

Katharine Parnell spent the rest of her life grieving for her husband, as her daughter Norah, who spent most of the rest of her life looking after Katharine, noted in a letter she wrote to Irish writer Henry Harrison on February 1, 1921, just four days before Katharine died. "She has never stopped mourning Parnell," wrote Norah.

Captain O'Shea, having succeeded in getting his hands on a portion of Katharine's inheritance following a vicious contest in probate court, spent the rest of his life living quietly and comfortably in southern England. He died in 1905.

Although Katharine O'Shea outlived Parnell by 30 years, she never recovered from the tragedy of his death. In 1921, her daughter Norah wrote in a letter that Katharine had "never stopped mourning Parnell" and that her profound sadness had brought her to the brink of insanity.

Neither the fact that Parnell's vision has not been realized nor the fact that his downfall, which was essentially of his own making, threw Irish politics into self-defeating disarray for almost a decade detracts from his achievements. No other Irish nationalist politician could have masterminded an agrarian agitation and a parliamentary agitation at the same time as effectively and brilliantly as Parnell; without Parnell, there would have been no Land Law (Ireland) Act passed in 1881. By turning home rule, which was little more than a vague aspiration entertained by a coterie of cautious lawyers when he entered politics, into a mighty cause backed by hundreds of thousands of Irishmen and one of the two major British political parties, Parnell transformed the entire basis of the relationship between Britain and Ireland, making it constructive where previously it had been hopelessly deadlocked.

The country that rejected Parnell eventually recognized that in casting out a man whom it had come to consider self-centered and dictatorial, it had thrown over a statesman who might one day have proven its savior. Parnell was, indeed, greatly missed by the country that had seen fit to judge him.

Parnell's brother and two of his sisters lay wreaths at his grave site. Several years later a massive boulder of Wicklow granite, marked simply PARNELL, was placed over the grave.

Further Reading

Bew, Paul. *Conflict and Conciliation in Ireland, 1890–1910: Parnellites and Radical Agrarians.* New York: Oxford University Press, 1987.

———. *C. S. Parnell.* Dublin: Gill & Macmillan, 1980.

Foster, R. F. *Charles Stewart Parnell: The Man and his Family.* Atlantic Highlands, NJ: Humanities Press, 1979.

Jackson, T. A. *Ireland Her Own: An Outline History of the Irish Struggle for National Freedom and Independence.* London: Cobbett Press, 1947.

Larkin, Emmet J. *The Roman Catholic Church in Ireland and the Fall of Parnell, 1888–1891.* Chapel Hill: University of North Carolina Press, 1979.

Lee, Joseph. *The Modernization of Irish Society 1848–1918.* Dublin: Gill & Macmillan, 1973.

Lyons, Francis Stewart Leland. *Charles Stewart Parnell.* Oxford: Oxford University Press, 1977.

———. *Culture and Anarchy in Ireland 1890–1939.* Oxford: Oxford University Press, 1979.

———. *Ireland Since the Famine.* London: Weidenfeld & Nicolson, 1971.

Murphy, William Michael. *The Parnell Myth and Irish Politics, 1891–1956.* New York: Peter Lang, 1986.

O'Brien, Conor Cruise. *Parnell and His Party 1880–1890.* Oxford: Oxford University Press, 1957.

O'Brien, Conor Cruise, and Marie O'Brien. *A Concise History of Ireland.* 3d ed. London: Thames & Hudson, 1985.

O'Brien R. Barry. *The Life of Charles Stewart Parnell 1846–1891.* 2 vols. 1898. Reprint (2 vols.). New York: Greenwood Press, 1969.

O'Day, Alan. *Parnell and the First Home Rule Episode, 1884–87.* Dublin: Gill and Macmillan, 1986.

O'Farrell, Patrick. *England and Ireland Since 1800.* Oxford: Oxford University Press, 1975.

O'Tuathaigh, Gearoid. *Ireland Before the Famine 1798–1848.* Dublin: Gill & Macmillan, 1972.

Chronology

June 27, 1846	Born Charles Stewart Parnell in Avondale, near Rathdrum, county Wicklow, Ireland
1859	John Parnell, father, dies at age 49; Charles inherits Avondale
1865	Parnell enrolls at Cambridge University, England
May 1869	Expelled from Cambridge; returns to Avondale
March 1875	Wins parliamentary by-election as Home Rule party candidate for county Meath
1877	Engages in his first parliamentary obstruction campaign with Joseph Biggar
Oct. 1879	Fenian Michael Davitt founds Irish National Land League (INLL), names Parnell president; land agitation initiated
May 17, 1880	Parnell elected chairman of Home Rule party
July 1880	Begins relationship with Katharine O'Shea
Oct. 1881	Arrested and imprisoned in Kilmainham Jail
May 2, 1882	Strikes Kilmainham Treaty with Prime Minister Gladstone; released from jail
May 6, 1882	Chief Secretary Cavendish and Under Secretary Burke assassinated in Phoenix Park, Dublin, by Irish National Invincibles
Sept. 1882	Parnell forms Irish National League (INL)
1885	Home Rule party wins 86 seats in general election, holds balance of power in House of Commons
June 8, 1886	Gladstone's Home Rule bill voted down in House of Commons
April 18, 1887	*Times* publishes forged letter implicating Parnell in Phoenix Park murders
Feb. 1889	Parnell cleared of all charges
Dec. 24, 1889	Captain O'Shea petitions for divorce; Parnell named as corespondent
Nov. 24, 1890	Gladstone demands Parnell's resignation
Dec. 6, 1890	Forty-four members of the Home Rule party secede
June 25, 1891	Parnell marries Katharine O'Shea
Oct. 6, 1891	Dies in Brighton, England

Index

John Haney graduated from London University in 1976 with an honors degree in classics. In recent years he has developed a special interest in history and political theory. A resident of New York City since 1982, he works as a writer, editor, musician, and lyricist. He is also the author of *Attlee* in this series.

Arthur M. Schlesinger, jr., taught history at Harvard for many years and is currently Albert Schweitzer Professor of the Humanities at City University of New York. He is the author of numerous highly praised works in American history and has twice been awarded the Pulitzer Prize. He served in the White House as special assistant to Presidents Kennedy and Johnson.

BIO   025222
PARNELL
          Haney, John
             Charles Stewart
Parnell

BIO   025222
PARNELL
          Haney, John
             Charles Stewart
Parnell

15 95

DATE	ISSUED TO